TENNIS
YOUR WAY

TENNIS YOUR WAY

by Nick Bollettieri

Illustrations By Joel Andrews

THE ATHLETIC INSTITUTE
200 Castlewood Drive
North Palm Beach, FL 33408

i

Library of Congress Catalog Card Number 82-73472
ISBN 0-87670-066-0

A Sports Publication by:
THE ATHLETIC INSTITUTE
Distributed by:
The Sporting News York
St. Louis, MO

TABLE OF CONTENTS

Acknowledgments . . . .
Foreword . . . .
Preface 2
Styles of Play 4
Evolution of the Racquet 7
Basics 12
Ready Position 19
The Forehand 22
    Beginning Forehand 22
    Straight Back Forehand 24
    Loop Forehand 26
    Forehand Weapon 30
The Backhand 34
    One-Hand Backhand 34
    Topspin Backhand 38
    Underspin Backhand 41
    Two-Handed Backhand 43
    Two-Handed with Release 47
The Volley 51
    Forehand and Backhand 51
    First Volley 55
    Shoulder Volleys 59
    Quick-Exchange Volley 62
    Half Volley 64
The Serve 67
    Basic Serve 71
    Intermediate Serve 74
    Advanced Serve 76
Overhead 81
Return of Service 87
Lob 92
Drop Shot 100
Approach Shots 106
Essentials to Your Game 110

Singles Strategy 115
Doubles Strategy 121
Playing Crucial Points 130
How to Practice 134
Disciplined Practice 136
Physical Conditioning 142
Appendix 158

ACKNOWLEDGMENTS

Throughout my life I have been fortunate in many ways. The good Lord blessed me with the talent for tennis instruction on all levels of play and an eye that lets me see a player's capabilities and weaknesses. Also I possess a natural dogmatic and motivating personality. This drive enables me to get my students to work at bettering their game while learning to enjoy the sport at the same time. For all of this, I am thankful.

Most important, however, I have been lucky enough to chance upon many great people who have supported and promoted my career and well being. While it would be impossible to thank everyone individually, I would like to acknowledge and express my deeply felt gratitude to some of the people who have been a continuous help to me over the years.

I owe a large debt to the entire Nick Bollettieri staff headed by director Larry Ware and including Steve Owens and Kathy Owens, Carolina Bolivar, Greg Bruenich, Chip Brooks and Gordon Kotinek. They have given me far more than their teaching talents to make the Nick Bollettieri Tennis Academy a success. I thank each and every one.

For its generous commitment to the overall development of the sport of tennis, a very special thanks to Subaru of America.

A very special thanks to Julio Moros and his beautiful family for their friendship and enduring loyalty.

Many thanks to my distinguished and enthusiastic managers Ralph Campbell, Donald Dell and David Handel.

For the endless nights of encouragement, along with many suggestions for the book, I thank Michael Patrick.

The N.B.T.A. students look forward to their time at the Academy, several students being there through the sponsorship of Atari.

And thanks to Dr. Murph Klauber, owner of the Colony Beach and Tennis Resort on Longboat Key, Florida, for giving me the opportunity to use the facilities to begin the Nick Bollettieri Tennis Academy.

For their overwhelming generosity and unsurpassed kinship, a very warm thanks to Mr. Nathan Landow, Mr. Monty Hurowitz, Mr. John Bassett, Mr. and Mrs. Samuel Reed and their families.

A special thanks to a very generous and loyal friend, Mr. Louis Marx and family.

Throughout the book I have listed the names of students who attended the Academy or camps and received instruction from me.

It would be impossible to credit all the vast numbers who were part of our program but I would like to personally thank the following and wish them continued success in tennis and in life.

A special note of thanks to supporters of the Academy:

Arthur Ashe: 15 years have passed since I started All American Camps. Arthur Ashe, along with many other touring pros, visited and helped me develop Jr. Camps. Throughout that time I have been fortunate to know Arthur as a person as well as admire his tennis ability. I can say nothing but "Arthur, you are #1." Looking forward to our clinics in the Far East and again, you are welcome to those great fish dinners; I will stick to rice and vegetables. Hello to Jeanne and my deepest appreciation for the financial support of our N.B.T.A. students.

Bill Shelton: now working with Pro Serve out of Washington, D.C., was previously associated with Prince Manufacturing as Player-Representative. Bill assists in all areas giving endless hours to Jr. development and guides possible pro players. He is a friend of 15 years.

Steve Contardi: I have the deepest respect for this long-time friend who worked as a director for me. He is currently directing two clubs: Harper's Point Racquet Club and The Lexington Tennis Club.

Tom Pucci: highly successful tennis coach at the University of Arkansas; his doubles team won the NCAA in 1982. His teams are always highly regarded.

Julie Anthony: Julie was a former student of mine and then co-authored "A Winning Combination." It would be impossible for me to find a more devoted and hard-working student than Julie. Hopefully, she will remain in sports for the rest of her life.

Brian Gottfried: who since age 10 has not only been a student of mine but a member of the Bollettieri family. All of the tennis world knows him for his fine sportsmanship and the dedication he has given to the tennis world. Formally ranked #4 singles player in the world; #1 doubles player for 3 years.

Chip Hooper: In 1980 upon the recommendation of Arthur Ashe and Tom Pucci of the University of Arkansas, Chip came to the Nick Bollettieri Tennis Academy to improve his groundstrokes. He returned to school after 6 months and won the NCAA Indoor. In November of 1981, he returned to the Academy; Chip had experienced 2 months of difficult times due to an eye operation. We sat and discussed what had to be done to reach his goals. At that time he was #248 on the computer and in order to reach his goals, it would require endless work both on and off the courts. Chip departed in mid-January very confident as we had worked considerably on a topspin backhand, underslice backhand and his first volley. Each day Bill Shelton would call offering encouragement and assuring Chip his tournament schedule was being taken care of. His first tournament was a major one, the Pro Indoors in Philadelphia. Chip, because of his ranking had to pre-qualify and qualify to get into the main draw. Not only did he accomplish that but reached the semi's losing to Connors in 4 sets. This tournament was the beginning of his climb to the top teens and low 20's in 6 months. Each time Chip returns to the Academy to brush up on his game, he works harder and harder. We all congratulate Chip!

Jimmy Arias: at 16 years old, he became the youngest male player ever to make the computer. A student for 4 years at the N.B.T.A. and currently ranked in the 70's; also won 1981 French Open mixed doubles with Andrea Jaeger. Jimmy has been a tremendous asset to the Academy and his big, semi-western loop forehand and big follow-through (taught by his father) have made a world-wide impact. Jimmy started at the age of 6 years. Jimmy's progress has been steady with several big wins; the next 18 months will be important in his development and climb to the top. The Bollettieri Family along with Carling and Danielle all miss Jimmy's 3 years living at our home.

Carling Bassett: at only 13 years of age, Carling was ranked very high in the 18 and under world rankings. She lost in the finals of the JAL Cup in 1982 to Zina Garrison. Carling is considered one of the best young pro prospects in the world. My entire family feels very close to Carling as she has been living at our home for 4 years; the house is very empty without her and my daughter Danielle. Danielle and Carling put that little something extra into home activities. (you never know what!)

Aaron Krickstein: The entire N.B.T.A. looks forward and is extremely excited to have Aaron become part of our team. He can do it all; watch for that name in the Pro ranks.

Martin Zumpft and Dierdre Herman: two 10 year olds with definite possibilities for becoming top players.

Susan Sloane: one of the best young girls I have had the opportunity to work with; winning the 12's National Indoors Championships, an outstanding player. Fritz Nau has worked with her several years doing an excellent job; we will work together to further develop her talents. Thanks, Fritz, for letting me help this outstanding young girl.

Shiho Okada: This young lady will spend the next 4 years of her life training at the N.B.T.A. At only 11 years old there is no doubt she will make a top player.

Lora Ann Baxley: student of mine, pro of mine, and is now enjoying a successful teaching job as pro in Little Rock, Arkansas. An outstanding young lady both on and off the court.

Pam Casale: When Pam, at 16 years of age, arrived at the Academy her strokes were very unorthodox. I didn't change them but worked within her style and added the volley and overhead along with the court strategy. This girl in one year moved into the top 20's. She is always a threat for a major upset. Pam's feet never stop moving . . . What a Girl!

Cary Cohenour: with his determination and natural ability he no doubt will be able to play college tennis for one of the best teams. If he continues to progress, he should be considered for the professional tour. At the Easter Bowl in 1981, he defeated the national champion, Al Parker, 6-2, 6-1.

Raffaella Reggi: a pleasure to work with; a girl whose personality is the very same on and off the court. She won the 1981 Orange Bowl, 16's girls beating Andrea Temesvari.

Ann White: was the first boarder at our Academy. Everyone should be as considerate as she is. Her success as a professional player shows her great playing ability.

Kathleen Horvath: while under my tutelage, she was the youngest girl ever to play in the U.S. Open and won almost every Jr. title of the United States and abroad. Although I no longer coach her, I respect her determination and wish her continued success.

Jose Lambert: he has developed into both a tremendous player and instructor. He is prepared to meet life's challenges because of his success in tennis; he is presently a student at the University of Arkansas.

The DePalmer Family: a super family; Mike, Sr. shared ownership of a tennis club in Bradenton, Florida. He is now coaching the University of Tennessee, attracting several young juniors. Mike, Jr. is now on the professional tour and returns to the Nick Bollettieri Tennis Academy for training. He was a member of the Junior Davis Cup Team, a collegiate All American and won the Jr. Doubles Championship with Rodney Harmon. He has been my pupil since the age of 12 and always gives 100%. Michelle enjoyed an outstanding junior and college career.

Rill and Tori Baxter: Rill is a fine college player for Pepperdine University. Tori is doing a great job with junior and pro development working with Prince Manufacturing. Tori gives endless hours of her personal time to help Jrs. and Pros both on and off the court.

Bill Quigley: an excellent junior player and now a fine college player at Brown University.

Eric Korita: playing great tennis for Southern Methodist University and has potential to become a touring professional.

Shlomo Glickstein: Israel's #1 player whom I had the opportunity to work with during the summers when he first came as a youngster to America.

Rodney Harmon: came to the Academy in January of 1979 with a ranking of #48; in 6 months it climbed to #4. In 1980, he won the Jr. doubles with Mike DePalmer and in 1981 he won the NCAA Doubles with Mel Purcell. There is no doubt he will become a top professional player; Rodney is very concerned for the welfare of all his friends. Arthur Ashe and Bill Shelton have contributed to his financial needs and tournament guidance.

Dana and Brad Gilbert: a fine college player and now a touring professional. Dana first came to the Academy in April; the past 6 months have been tough for her. In just 2 months she has climbed 50 spots on the computer. We both feel this is just the beginning; she works 24 hours per day. Brad was a finalist at 1982 NCAAs and now playing on the professional tour. He has outstanding athletic ability and will be a threat to many Pros in a short time.

Ron Hightower: excellent college player at Arkansas and now playing on the professional tour. He is very considerate to young Jrs. and helps whenever and wherever needed.

John Levine: came in his Sr. year. His attitude and willingness to accept small adjustments was very negative. By the end of his stay his personality had become more positive and appreciative. His results at the University of Texas and on the Penn Circuit are outstanding.

Tom Fontana: was a very dedicated and hard worker while attending the Academy. His results at the University of Texas speak for themselves, excellent!

Stephan Eggmayer: Stephan came to the Academy on the recommendation of Dennis Ralston. Dennis felt that the Academy would toughen Stephan mentally and physically. Many hours were spent developing his topspin groundstrokes and forcing volleys. Today Stephan is playing competitive tennis in Germany and is ranked high in the world junior rankings.

I would like to give a special note of thanks to the following:
Jack Murray and Howard Head of Prince Manufacturing
Robert Kaplan and Gabriele Brustenghi of Ellesse
Roberto Muller and Chester Wheeler of Pony
Alan Ross, Harvey Lamm, and Audrey Wilner of Subaru
John Plimpton and David Grant of Penn
Steve Ross and Mike Martin of Atari

Because of the vast number of outstanding juniors and college players, it would be impossible to list all of them separately; below is a list of students who have attended the Academy and helped in its success.

Ira Schwartz	University of Miami
Moe Krueger	University of S.C.
Susan Jarrell	S.M.U.
Chris Green	CA
Julie and Beth Rupert	University of KY, Vanderbilt
Paul Annacone	University of TN
Arthur Heller	University of S.C.
Mark Bailey	University of KY
Matt Halder	University of KY
Patricia Shaw	Arkansas
Darren Roberts	University of S.C.
Lori Kosten	University of TN
Barrett Powers	Rutgers

Last, but most important, I want to express my affectionate and heartfelt appreciation to my family. Without their patience, love and understanding, this book would never have been possible. Thank you Mom, Dad, Rita, Jimmy, Dani, Angel and my best friend and wife, Kellie.

Nick Bollettieri

FOREWORD

As a kid, I was encouraged (some say "forced") to read books on tennis. My teacher, Dr. R.W. Johnson, thought Bill Tilden's **The Spin Of The Ball** was the definitive work on our sport. But that was back in 1953.

Obviously, we now need new definitions. Equipment changes — racquets, balls, etc. — have made everyone re-think Tilden's "that it takes five years to make a tennis player and ten years to make a champion." Tracy Austin, Kathy Rinaldi, Mats Wilander, and Bjorn Borg have laid that dictum to rest.

Nick Bollettieri is probably our best known tennis teacher of intermediate and advanced junior players. I can say two things about Nick: he is different and he gets results.

So what makes this book different? "The Lesson" section, which forms an integral part of each chapter, puts you in the position of the pupil. In other words, given the limitations of not being physically present, the questions asked in "The Lesson" section are questions that you would ask yourself.

No two tennis teaching pros would give the same kind of instruction. There is no such thing as "the" right way to hit a forehand or a backhand. Somehow though, Nick gets results — time and time again.

His book would be a welcome addition to your tennis library.

Arthur R. Ashe

PREFACE

Before going into the specific suggestions that will help your game, let's establish the pattern of this book.

First, I will explain every avenue of your style of play, taking into consideration grips, footwork, mobility, goals, experience, mental attitude, court strategy and physical conditioning. Through a series of simple lessons, we will try to make improvements in your game. I have included student dialogue in some of these lessons in the hope that you may benefit from their comments or questions.

Second, I will not suggest any changes in your game unless you understand what is to be done. I will suggest alterations in your game if they are feasible and if it is what you want.

However, if you do select a change, I urge you to be patient. Often, in order to reach a higher level of play you must back up. Learning a new method takes time and while you perfect the technique you may have to accept a slight reversal in your game. Remember, to make a long-time gain often requires a short-time loss.

(NOTE: Quite often I will attempt small changes without discussing it with you. But if a grip change is required, it must become a point of discussion between you and your tennis pro.)

Third, no matter what aspect of the game we're discussing: stroke production, footwork, mental attitude, etc., I will work with you on a very simple basis. I do not believe the majority of students need complicated methods to explain what should be a simple change in their game.

Through my book I will demonstrate how simple it can be to add a new stroke without the student being aware of a change. Since all strokes are basically the same except for the position of the racquet head on contact, it is quite easy to build new shots on old skills. But, though the changes will be subtle, there will probably be discomfort, pain and some mental strain in the process. Even those who have developed calloused hands from hours of practice will reach for a Bandaid when I make a small adjustment to their grip. Ben Gay and a whirlpool treatment are often needed when players are asked to extend their serving arm up and out when making contact with the ball.

Julie Anthony, co-author of our book, ''A Winning Combination,'' wrote several chapters on the pro-student-parent relationship. There are many suggestions in that book for improving that association. However, there is one particular chapter, ''Coaching Tips For Mind and Body,'' that I will refer to frequently.

Finally, I realize that most players do not like to make changes in their game. Too often, after a few weeks they don't maintain the new methods and slip back into old familiar patterns.

But remember, nothing comes without patience and practice. Quite often I hear students remark that a new grip or shot just doesn't feel natural. What they don't consider is that the old way seemed ''natural'' because it was the method they always used, and secondly, just because it felt right didn't make it the best way. Keeping in mind that learning new techniques may be difficult and produce uneasiness, it is important that you practice the changes until they too seem natural.

I won't tell you that you're going to go from being a modest player to a champion in just a short period. Work and practice is required no matter on what level you participate. This is a realistic book — not a miracle cure. This book will not go into depth on body movements, rotation of hips and shoulders or exact angles of the racquet face on contact. What this book will do is give a series of simple lessons that should help you correct, learn or improve your game.

One final note. Throughout this book, all instruction and examples will be for right-handed players. A lefty does exactly the same except for the playing hand.

1

STYLES OF PLAY

Classical

Basically, in the late 50s and early 60s, good tennis players used the classical strokes with the following characteristics:
1. The Eastern Forehand.
2. The Eastern Backhand.
3. Continental volley grip — for the occasional trip to the net.
4. Continental or Eastern Backhand service grip.

If you happened to be watching a match during this era, you were very often likely to hear the following tips for the aspiring player:
1. Hit through the ball.
2. Point your racquet exactly where you want the ball to go and not another inch.
3. Never hit a ball with an open stance!
4. Put your free hand on the throat of the racquet to help guide your backhand.
5. Develop conservative ground strokes and only run around the forehand or backhand when the ball is down the middle — then go to your stronger side.
6. Never stroke the volley — just punch the ball.
7. Don't jump — bend the knees and stay down.
8. Don't overhit the ball — just put it back in play.

9. Develop your backhand rather than running around it to hit a forehand.
10. Don't hit the ball high above the net or you'll be lobbing too often.

Of course times have changed and so has the game. Through the years I have taught many students from all parts of the world and with all levels of talent and the one thing I've learned is to be flexible. No longer is the rigid ''classical style'' the only way to play. There are many different but successful methods.

In teaching I attempt to offer simple suggestions to add to a person's game without changing his individual style. Only after this method has been exhausted will I make major alterations or changes in the grip.

Although there are certain guidelines for good stroke production, especially evident in the backswings on groundstrokes, no two people will hit the ball the same. These individual traits will not be changed — only adjusted to maximize performance.

To illustrate how varied styles can be effective, consider some of the top players in the world today and how they have achieved success following different paths.

Bjorn Borg's topspin percentage game has brought many Wimbledon titles. Jimmy Connors uses a hard-hitting attack from all parts of the court to win his share of championships. Gene Mayer has risen to the top using a large racquet and great ball control. Ivan Lendl uses a Semi-Western grip and blazing groundstrokes to achieve devastating shots.

And don't forget the classical styles of the successful Arthur Ashe and Brian Gottfried or the magic feet and Western Forehand of Harold Solomon. Roscoe Tanner uses a low toss on the serve while another left-hander, John McEnroe takes a closed stance though both have devastating serves.

The stars of tomorrow have unique styles too. Two of my male students are both successful using different techniques. Jimmy Arias booms forehand and backhand groundstrokes while Chip Hooper humbles his opposition with a fierce serve and volley attack.

On the women's tour different styles of play are just as obvious. The steady graceful baseline attack of Chris Evert Lloyd and Tracy Austin is contrasted with the powerful serve and volleys of Martina Navratilova and the superb shot making of Hana Mandlikova. Andrea Jaeger has a potent two-handed backhand and an effective moon ball which allows her to control her opponents while Pam Shriver uses an uncanny reach at the net to win.

Like the male students, I have several successful women who use their own style. Pam Casale, currently ranked in the top twenty-five, uses an unorthodox style which suits her game while Carling Bassett and Raffaella Reggi use great feet and daring net play to win their matches.

All of the players mentioned have unique and different styles. All are winners but few look the same on the court. It would not only be impossible but totally impractical to attempt to have all these players conform to a single grip, backswing or follow-through. The point is, tennis players are individuals and my staff and I have had to be open and flexible with our teaching methods. It is this flexibility in our instruction which has enabled us to develop a student's game within his style of play.

2

EVOLUTION OF THE RACQUET

As a teaching pro, I am often asked: "Which racquet is best for me?"

This is a tricky question, because no single racquet suits everyone; at my junior academy I would guess almost every model on the market is in the hands of this or that student. There simply is no "magic wand" to make someone an outstanding player overnight. It is my experience that if two players compete against each other, and one wins decisively, the results would be the same in a rematch even if they switched racquets.

This is not to say certain racquets will not suit you better than others. The best racquet is the one in which you have confidence. If something "feels" right in your hand, and if it works for you, go with it regardless of outside influences. Too often people are swayed by what the pros are using. You should keep several things in mind when you see a top professional walk onto the court carrying an armful of racquets.

The first is that he or she is given equipment free, so price is no object. Nor does it concern them if the racquets have a tendency to break, warp or quickly lose string tension. Also the pro is often paid huge sums of money to use a firm's racquets.

There is no question equipment can make a difference, however, especially in view of the strides made in racquet construction in the last decade. Modern technology has changed the look of tennis dramatically. Many people believe the biggest single advance occurred in the late 1970s when oversized racquets were introduced.

The man who developed oversized racquets is Howard Head, a fellow I have come to know over the years. One of Head's favorite pastimes is playing poker; obviously he enjoys a gamble, and as he has fiddled with a variety of inventions the man has come up with more than his share of winners. It took him three years and more than 40 different designs but he eventually produced the first aluminum ski, one that was stronger, livelier and three times more resistant to twisting than the old wood models.

Years later, retired from the ski business and trying to use up the hours in the day around his home in Baltimore, Howard was a frustrated tennis player who had spent $5000 on tennis lessons and had yet to find the way to put some "ping" into his game — ping being the beguiling sound made when the ball hits the racquet squarely. Just as he had with his skis, Head visited his basement workshop where he began experimenting with disastrous results. The racquets kept breaking. Finally, it came to him. "Make it bigger," he said. So it was developed by a man new to tennis, and thus a fellow free of its traditional notions. When he was finished, he had a racquet with a hitting area of approximately 110 square inches, so Head nicknamed his new weapon the 110.

The big selling point of the racquet is those added square inches of hitting area that turn mis-hit thuds into a sweet ping — the racquet has 50 percent more hitting area than a conventional model. But another advantage is that the 110 has less twist to it on off-center hits, and less potentially damaging vibration traveling up the arm. The player thus has more control, and its proponents hope that the bigger racquets will help solve the problem of injuries to elbows and shoulders caused by vibrations from off-center hits.

The increased and better sweet spot, as well as the improved stability were enough to convince the U.S. Patent Office to grant Howard Head a patent on his racquet that will be good until 1993. This patent covers racquets made with a hitting area between 85 and 130 square inches, and it explains the birth of another popular racquet: the mid-size. This racquet is a direct result of the patent since its hitting area is smaller, by a millimeter or two, than 85 square inches.

Almost from the beginning, some of the results people got from the larger racquets bordered on the spectacular and caused many people, including myself, to re-examine their views on equipment. Imagine what an impact it would make in baseball if suddenly a player could be given a bat with almost four times the hitting area. Or if a basketball player could shoot at a hoop that was appreciably larger than the one at which his opponents were shooting. Basically, that is what happened in tennis when the 110s debuted.

In the early going, one of the biggest success stories was Gene Mayer, a fellow who was not nearly the best player on his college team at Stanford University. As a pro, Gene was not doing much either. He was ranked 148th in the world when he picked up a 110. Some time later, he was ranked fourth. Obviously he had confidence in his equipment. He believed in it. It was a winning combination.

Another case is Vince Van Patten, son of actor Dick Van Patten. Vince came out of Hollywood with a two-fisted backhand and a 110 and began a fast rise several years ago. In late 1981 he won the Seiko tournament in Japan, beating John McEnroe along the way. No wonder Eric Van Dillen, a former All-America and U.S. Davis Cup player has predicted that within two years 90 percent of the players will have switched from the traditionally sized racquet.

Some years ago I can remember talking to a professional player who at the time was ranked about 100th in the world. He was upset because he had been defeated in a tournament by a player using an oversize racquet. "They should outlaw those things," the pro said. I could not believe it. Here was a pro, a man whose career hinged on playing tennis for prize money, and he was admitting that large racquets gave someone an advantage. I didn't dispute his reasoning. With larger racquets your chances of making those stretched out volleys, or reaching overheads and of hitting shots on the run have to improve. It is simple geometry; those balls that hit off the frame of a traditional racquet wind up on the strings of an oversized. Talking to the pro, however, I could not understand why if he thought the bigger racquets were better, he was not using one himself. He had a reverse confidence problem: He believed in his opponent's equipment more than he did his own.

I have to admit that when oversized racquets first started showing up some years back, I did not like them. There were several reasons. The first was a cosmetic objection, tinged with a bit of stubbornness. After a lifetime of using a traditional racquet, the new models seemed huge to me even though with my eyes closed I could not feel any difference. Early on, most people called the 110s "flyswatters." Tennis is a traditional game and I respect tradition as much as the next fellow. But suddenly it was as if the rules were being changed, although tacitly, to allow new, mammoth racquets that looked as if they belonged in the grasp of Paul Bunyon.

But actually, the rules always have been quite liberal in regard to the size and shape of a racquet. Over the years there have been experiments with racquets bent to resemble a pitchfork, or with a rectangularly shaped head; Richard Sears used such a model to win the first national championship in 1881. Almost comically, there even was one racquet designed with a ventilated handle that came complete with a tiny, battery-powered fan inside to keep one's hand dry. So, given the latitude of the rules, the 110 was an invention, more or less, waiting to happen.

Originally, my other objection to the 110 was a bit more realistic. For me, the first racquets on the market did not accomplish much. The early 110s were much too flexible; there was a trampoline effect with the ball more or less ricocheting off the racquet face. Now racquets are produced out of a variety of substances; aluminum, graphite, even wood, so there is a degree of flexibility and feel to suit everyone's game, from the baseliner to the fellow with a cannonball serve. The manufacturers also have discovered the big racquets need to be strung tighter, usually to around 80 pounds of pressure. This has solved the problem of the ball trampolining off the face.

How much of an impact have the big racquets made? Let's put it this way. Every player in the world, beginning with Bjorn Borg, John McEnroe and Ivan Lendl, has been beaten at one time or another by someone using an oversize racquet. The flyswatters have become giant killers. Some people prefer the mid-size, some the oversize. But it seems certain the trend is towards bigger racquets and away from the traditional ones.

True, players such as John McEnroe, Bjorn Borg and Ivan Lendl all use regular size racquets. Obviously they are getting high performance from their equipment. You should stay with the traditional size too if you think you can hit the ball on the sweet spot time after time the way the top players do. Actually, the best players such as McEnroe, Borg, etc., use equipment because of loyalty and familiarity; when they first learned the game, there was only one size racquet. Howard Head was still tinkering in his basement. A look at the junior ranks, however, where the 110 seems by far to be the most popular racquet, or at the pro satellite circuits, where the same is true, shows that the direction of player acceptance is toward the mid-size and 110-size racquets.

Although I hesitate to unequivocally say the racquets are for everyone, obviously I lean toward the bigger racquet. I believe that with the research and improved construction that has taken place in recent years, every player can suit his needs with the new equipment. My advice would be to give the racquet a fair chance: one man's Ferrari is another's Volkswagen and you cannot learn how a car handles by just starting it up. Give the racquet a reasonable tryout.

One brief note of caution. If you are accustomed to playing with traditional equipment, you will find that there is a slightly different technique to using the mid- and 110-size models because the sweet spot is located more towards the throat of the racquets rather than at their center. But once you get the hang of it, you probably will be just like me and make the switch. It is interesting to note that while a lot of players are converting over to the bigger racquets, you do not see very many going back the other way. Indeed every major manufacturer is now producing an oversize or mid-size racquet.

3

BASICS

Selection of a Proper Sized Racquet

Before you can begin improving your game, first you have to have proper equipment. The racquet, of course, is the most important instrument in the game and care should be taken when making your selection.

The use of large heavy racquets with equally massive grips has changed because of the number of younger players. Now the majority of equipment is smaller and lighter and for the most part, evenly balanced. Most players today select a racquet with a grip size of 4-3/8 to 4-1/2 inches and a light to medium weight.

My suggestion is to use a racquet that feels comfortable to you. Select a grip size that you can control and one that does not weigh too much for effective use. With manufacturers offering such a wide variety of sturdy, lightweight racquets, no one should have trouble finding the perfect balance between grip size and weight.

The following are simple guides in selecting a racquet:

1. Have a qualified teaching professional or a knowledgeable sales person help you make your selection. Expert advice can help assure you get a racquet suited for you — and save you money as well.

2. Shake hands with the racquet handle and be able to insert the first finger of your opposite hand between your finger and thumb.

The Grip

Regardless of what type grip you use, this is where your tennis game really begins. There have always been opinions and arguments as to which grip is best, but the most important consideration is which grip is **best for you.** It is imperative to find the one best suited for you, keeping in mind the variables such as power, control and the ability to be consistent. While the grip is fundamental to the game most players know very little about it, though to a large extent it will determine the style of play.

There are four important elements to remember about grips:

1. No matter how you make your backswing, follow-through, or preparation the **GRIP IS CONSTANT.**

2. No matter which grip you choose, in the beginning it may seem awkward or feel uncomfortable.

3. Except for underspin shots, the face of the racquet is vertical when it makes contact with the ball. Since the grip will determine the position of your wrist when stroking the ball, certain grips will make it more difficult to get into the proper position.

4. Youngsters have a higher degree of variation in their grips because of a lack of strength and discipline. Normally, a beginning child will feel more secure in a Semi or Western grip which has the hand holding the racquet very much like a baseball bat with the palm underneath the handle.

The Eastern Forehand Grip

This grip seems to be the most adaptable for the majority of players. I feel, if given no other choice, the Eastern Forehand would allow most players on all levels of skill, to compete and hit all balls with the least amount of adjustment.

Eastern Forehand

The following are important elements of this grip:

1.   With the palm of your hand placed on the backside of the handle, pretend you are shaking hands with the racquet. This movement will form an Eastern Forehand grip. The palm of the hand and the racquet handle should be vertical at all times.

2.   Another method of correctly mastering this grip is to place the hitting hand in the face of the racquet while holding the throat with the free hand. Slide your hand down the handle and again shake hands.

3.   When you have a correct grip, your thumb and first finger will form a ''V.''

4.   It is important to spread your fingers apart slightly because this will give you greater control of the racquet.

5.   The thumb should be between the first and second finger and around the handle.

The Eastern Backhand

The Eastern Forehand and Eastern Backhand are grips that can be used to hit any type shot and it is easy to switch from one to the other. This grip offers maximum stability and the position of the palm and fingers requires very little wrist adjustment on the forward part of the swing to get the racquet face vertical for contact. Another aspect of this grip is the ability to impart topspin to the ball by hitting from a low to a high point with a firm wrist and a brushing motion on contact.

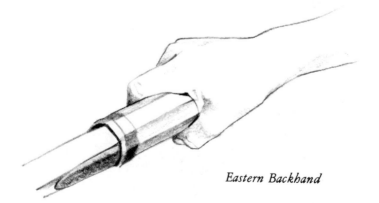

Eastern Backhand

The following are important elements of this grip:

1. Hold the throat of your racquet with your free hand while you move your hitting hand (not the racquet) approximately one-quarter turn to the left. The thumb and index finger will form a "V" along the left top level of the handle.

2. Hold the racquet head perpendicular to the ground and shake hands with the lower part of the handle, making sure the heel of your hitting hand is on the right level and your thumb pad is on the left level. The position of the thumb will vary according to individual comfort and strength.

3. An optional method of hand positioning for this shot is to place the thumb on a diagonal line across the backside of the handle as far underneath as possible. Place it between the index finger, which is spread slightly, and the third finger.

The Continental

The predominant playing surface throughout Europe and South America is slow clay, which produces a low bounce. The Continental grip is adapted to this height without trouble, though it is difficult to use on high bouncing balls — especially those hit with power and depth — because the palm is directly on top of the racquet, making it hard to control the vertical angle on contact.

The Continental grip is sometimes called the "lazy player's" grip because no change is required from forehand to backhand. But there are many limitations to this grip unless you are very strong and talented. Rod Laver and Lew Hoad use this grip but both were capable of making proper wrist adjustments on contact to maintain control. Too often, inexperienced players can not.

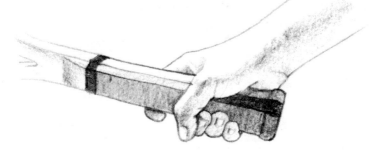

Continental

The following are important elements of this grip:

1. The "V" of your index finger and thumb will be in the middle of the Eastern Forehand and Eastern Backhand for correct Continental grip. The palm of the hand is directly on top of the racquet.

2. Beginners, the majority of women and numerous men who lack strength should avoid this grip.

3. It is essential to meet the ball in front of you to maintain correct positioning of the wrist. If this is not done, ball control will decrease.

4. Because the palm is on top of the racquet, it is much harder to push the handle forward on contact — especially when the ball gets behind you.

5. It is very difficult to hit crosscourt forehands when running far to your right with this grip.

The Semi-Western/Full Western

The Semi-Western grip originated in California where most playing surfaces, until recently, were hard cement. A characteristic of this court is high bouncing balls which the Semi-Western grip can accommodate. This grip establishes the hitting palm around the right side of the grip and at the same time gives added strength.

Many players use this Semi-Western grip, including Borg, Dibbs, Clerc, Vilas and Ivan Lendl.

The Full Western grip, used by Harold Solomon among others, is very similar except that the palm of the hitting hand is partially underneath the handle of the racquet on contact. I do not recommend the Full Western for most players, but prefer an extreme Eastern Forehand to Semi-Western grip which all levels can adopt.

One of my students, Jimmy Arias, uses the Semi-Western. Jimmy, who has been playing since he was six years old and introduced to the game with this grip, by his father, produces a lot of power and topspin with his wrist acceleration on contact. Trying to accomplish this action with a Continental or Eastern Forehand grip would be very difficult.

The following are important elements of the Full Western/Semi-Western Grips:

1. This grip offers strength because of the position of the palm. Youngsters especially feel very secure with this grip because it adds strength and, hopefully, control.

2. When in a Full Western and even Semi-Western, it is difficult to hit low forehands because of a tendency for the rac-

Western

Semi-Western Forehand

quet face to close very quickly. Often the ball is smothered into the net.

Semi-Western Backhand

This is a grip which has gained popularity in the past three or four years and is currently being used effectively by Lendl, Clerc and others. Even though I teach this grip, I cannot really recommend it unless you feel very comfortable with it.

Butch Bueholz was an outstanding player in the late 60s and early 70s. He used this grip very effectively. However, he feels it placed so much stress on his elbow area it contributed to the operations and tennis elbow problem he developed.

The following are important elements of the Semi-Western Backhand:

1. Adopt an Eastern Backhand grip then slide your hand one-eighth to one-quarter turn to your left while your fingers close together in an apparent hammer grip. It is exactly the same as a Semi-Western Forehand on the opposite side. (Illustration.)

2. This grip produces a great deal of topspin but requires strength to control it.

Semi-Western Backhand

4

READY POSITION

The ready position is the building block upon which groundstrokes, serves, overheads and volleys are built. Sloppy beginnings lead to poor results and for this reason a proper ready position is stressed early and often in lessons with all my students.

Having worked with thousands of students I have concluded everyone starts out with their own ready position. There is no single method to use for all students because to be effective, the ready position relies on personal preferences.

Yet even though every ready position will vary, there are essential points you must adopt in your method.

Don't be afraid to experiment if you're not satisfied with your ready position but remember the key points are constant.

The following are the Key Points of the Ready Position:

1. Concentrate on the ball at all times.
2. Be relaxed and ready to move in any direction.
3. During the ready position, hold the racquet in your left hand so you can make grip changes or pull it back when moving to the ball.
4. Be positive. Concentrate on getting to every ball.
5. Study your opponent. You may be able to determine where his shots are going.

19

The Lesson

Nick — *Geoffrey, I am pleased with your stroke production and the way you play points. But there is one part of your game which cost you your last tournament. The addition of a basic fundamental could have helped you win the match or at least have given you better results.*

Geoffrey — *Tell me what it is.*

Nick — *Let's rally from the baseline and see if you can determine the missing link.*

Geoffrey — *Give me a hint.*

Nick — *It is not directly related to your strokes but it always affects the outcome. During our rallies, try to figure out why you hit your balls in the vicinity of my service line and why you have difficulty hitting crosscourts when running wide.*

Geoffrey — *I must be having a great day today. This is the best control I've ever had and my feet just won't stop moving.*

Nick — *You can do it every day if you concentrate on every ball and are prepared for the ball before it crosses the net. Your ready position is the key to the entire game.*

Geoffrey — *What's wrong with my ready position?*

Nick — *Nothing today. That's because you're excited and you're concentrating before my serves. But you do what a lot of people do during a match. You forget to concentrate on this basic element of play.*

During your last tournament you were standing up too straight and the racquet was too close to your body. Also, you did not pick up the ball until it bounced on your side. Of course, that's too late.

In order to position yourself to make effective returns, you must be reacting to the ball before it clears the net. You can only do that when you concentrate and develop the traits of a sound ready position.

Conclusion

Everyone has to decide what is going to work best for them. But unless you are prepared with the fundamentals of a sound ready position, you will constantly struggle from a position of weakness.

Like everything else in tennis, getting used to a ready position takes practice. And the lack of concentration during practice is the cause of many unforced errors in actual play.

It is essential to get a quick body turn and first step in the direction of the ball. Quickness is the key.

But it's like the old childhood saying: **Get Ready. Get Set. Go!**

Before you can move to win a point, you must first get ready. When you practice, include the key points to a sound ready position in your game. Make them a habit and you will improve.

5

THE FOREHAND

Beginning Forehand

There are and always will be several different approaches to start teaching a basic beginner. Throughout my career I have taught thousands of beginners at municipal parks, tennis camps and country clubs and the one thing I've learned is that a coach has got to be flexible. No two people have the same abilities and no two beginners are going to respond identically to the same instruction.

But, while I always encourage my beginners — and my advanced students as well — to seek the method which is most natural, I still maintain certain points that are fundamental to those just learning the game.

In the following simulated lessons, I'll attempt to show how I stress certain key points to a beginner while searching for clues to their own natural style of play.

The Forehand

The forehand is a basic stroke in tennis. It should be taught to the beginning students as simply as possible — the less complicated the better. Some students can do wonderful things by themselves. Others need more stringent guidelines. Until I know which type the student is, I allow as much flexibility as possible.

While I'm starting the forehand lesson, I also begin work on the backhand. Some coaches prefer to teach them separately. But I feel they should be taught alongside one another. Both shots are important and I don't like students to get the impression one is more valuable or more difficult than the other. After the student develops, one shot will become more dominant, but from the beginning I stress them both.

Finally, I firmly believe that the Semi-Western grip on the forehand is the optimum stroke for the beginning student. It provides strength and will lend itself nicely to developing a big forehand later on. Unless the student shows a marked preference for another grip, I encourage the use of this method.

These are five points to remember in the beginning forehand lesson:

1. Good ready position.
2. Get the racquet head back quickly.
3. Hit smoothly and not for power.
4. Watch the ball.
5. Hit from a low to a high point with a long follow-through.

The Lesson

Nick — *Lindsey, the first thing I want to say is the most important lesson to learn today — or any other day — to enjoy the game of tennis. Without enjoyment, learning anything is more difficult.*

We'll be working hard today, but while we're here I want you to try your hardest. No matter how you play, if you give me a 100 percent effort, I'll be satisfied.

First, the racquet you're using has three major parts: the grip, the throat and the racquet head. To get the proper grip, hold the racquet in the throat of your left hand and slide your right hand down the throat and shake hands. Now turn your hand a little to the right. Look at the position of your hand but don't worry about it. You're now using the Semi-Western grip.

I'll toss you some balls to hit while you concentrate on keeping your eyes on the ball, getting your racquet head back quickly and following through after you swing. And remember, power isn't everything. It certainly isn't the key to winning.

You're doing fine. Now let's hit a few backhands and see how you do.

Lindsey — *My mother told me the forehand would require several lessons before the backhand started.*

Nick — *Your mom did not tell you wrong, but there are lots of different ways of teaching. I'd like you to be comfortable hitting both shots. And since you mentioned it, I'm pleased your mother has an interest in your game. She is very important in your tennis development and I think she should know what we're doing. Why don't you see if she can come and watch our next lesson. She may be surprised at what you can do from the very beginning.*

Conclusion

Not much else need be said to the beginning student until he or she starts to develop. Footwork, body rotation and placement all come in time and by small steps after the student gains confidence.

As I said, the backhand is important and should be taught with the forehand. After seeing the beginner hit a few balls, I suggest either an Eastern Backhand grip or a two-handed backhand with any grip. Again, I'm searching for natural tendencies.

Whatever you do, as a beginning student, don't try to learn everything at one time. Work in small areas and learn good fundamentals. If you work on your game in this manner you will be less likely to become frustrated.

Straight Back Forehand and Follow-Through

To a large extent, the backswing determines the success or failure of the stroke. Whatever style you select will require practice to overcome the danger points.

Both the straight back swing and the loop backswing are correct. I will not force a student who is just beginning to adopt either way. It is better if they use the method which is most natural, although I will urge them to use a circular backswing as they advance. However, many of my advanced students start with and end up with the straight back method, which is actually half a loop. I do not teach a true straight back. If I did, the racquet would appear to be going back down toward the ground before the forward part of the swing would begin.

It makes no difference which style you use. What is important is that you begin the backswing the second you determine what stroke you will use. Wait too long before making this decision and you'll find yourself losing more than winning. In this case, quickness counts more than selection.

There are nine points to remember in the straight back forehand method:

Straight Back Forehand

1. Take the racquet straight back from the ready position.
2. Do not drop or raise the head.
3. Let the racquet head go back first.
4. Keep the backswing compact with the racquet head pointed toward the back fence.
5. On the forward swing, allow the racquet to go below the ball and don't muscle the stroke.
6. Follow through high — the arm should be relaxed and natural.
7. Your shoulders should rotate when you take the racquet back and open again on the forward part of the swing.
8. Get your racquet back as soon as you know it's a forehand.
9. Always have a long follow-through.

The Lesson

Nick — *Louis, I really feel we have accomplished a great deal with your forehand backswing. At this point the extra motions are just about out of your backswing. Remember that a flaw in your backswing can cause a major problem on the forward part of the stroke. The two are related.*

Louis — *For the past few months I have concentrated on taking my racquet head back in the straight back method but there are times when I am still late in meeting the ball in front.*

Nick — *From the simple ready position your racquet head goes back first, trying to keep the racquet head on the same height as the original ready position. I stand on the service line and volley your forehands. I am sure a little adjustment will help solve the problem.*

Louis — *When the balls are hit fairly slow everything seems fine but that last tournament was on a lightning-fast court and I did terribly.*

Nick — *There it is. You're dragging your racquet head on the backswing. In both the straight back and circular backswing the racquet head should start the backswing. You start your swing with the elbow and at the same time drop your racquet head to a low position. By doing this you have lost a split second needed to offset the hard forehand drives and serves hit at you.*

Louis — *You're probably right, but how can I stop that?*

Nick — *From your ready position take the racquet head back on the same level as your ready position. Keep your right elbow fairly close to your body until the racquet head is opposite your right shoulder and then extend the arm away from your body. Let's try a few more to make sure you have it down to a "T."*

Great, great, what a difference.

Louis — *The adjustment was so simple I must be stupid not to know that myself.*

Nick — *You're not stupid. Try to go back to basics if you experience difficulty. Remember, the racquet head leads the backswing.*

Conclusion

You cannot separate the backswing from the follow-through. The backswing has a major influence on the other.

1. From the ready position the racquet head leads the backswing.
2. Eliminate all extra motions, especially the elbow going back first or dropping the racquet head far below the ball at the very beginning of the swing.

Loop Forehand and Follow-Through

There are several methods of getting your racquet back into position for your shots, but one you should be familiar with is the loop.

The loop is a continuous circular motion, popular with many of today's leading players, that helps in timing and in the generation of topspin on the forehand side. This does not mean the straight backswing is not capable of topspin but, having worked with so many students, it seems to me a little more natural with the loop because of the continuous motion.

In addition to the small circular backswing I encourage my students to follow through way beyond the contact point. In fact, the follow-through should be limited only by whatever is natural. If the arm bends at the elbow and the racquet finishes around the left shoulder, it's fine with me.

To stop the racquet suddenly after contact takes a great deal of muscle. Not only could this lead to strain on the arm, but halting the follow-through prevents a natural swing which should be the primary concern.

There are four elements to a loop forehand and follow-through:

1. Use your free hand to push the racquet head up as soon as you see the ball coming to the forehand.
2. Have a continuous motion.
3. Keep the loop compact.
4. Follow through in a natural motion even if your racquet ends up around your shoulder.

Semi-Western Loop Forehand

The Lesson

Nick — *Jimmy, you have a great forehand but I think we can even make it better. In order to improve your forehand we're actually going to work on your backswing. I want you to stand inside the baseline a few steps while I volley hard at your feet. You'll have to start your backswing very quickly in order to be ready to hit a return.*

Jimmy, you're a little late on your shots. Cut down on the height of your loop backswing. Don't let the racquet head go above your shoulder. If it's too high you will experience difficulty in hitting crosscourts and controlling the ball.

Jimmy — *If you let me go back behind the baseline, I'll have more time for my backswing.*

Nick — *No, you can do it right there. You need quicker reactions. If you start sooner and cut the loop in half you'll have plenty of time. That's it. You've gotten rid of a lot of wasted motion and saved yourself some time. Your racquet head is now getting under the ball on the forward*

*Semi-Western
Loop Forehand*

part of your swing and that is adding control and topspin. Start your loop (circular motion) by pushing the racquet head up with your left hand.

Your follow-through also looks good. Your elbow is moving away from your body on the forward part of your stroke and you have a relaxed, natural swing. I think you'll find that if you move back behind the baseline now you'll notice a big difference. You'll have a lot of time to set up for your shots with the continuous relaxed motion and use a lot less energy to hit the ball. Results will certainly follow with practice.

Conclusion

When time is crucial, start your backswing the moment you see the ball approaching. Keep your racquet in a continuous motion of your loop swing and as the ball nears you, speed it up and let it drop down and under the ball.

Keep your arm relaxed and follow through with a natural motion. Don't worry about stopping after contact. Let the racquet head continue the follow-through to your natural stopping position.

Loop Forehand

The Forehand Weapon

Technological advancements are being made almost on a daily basis. Everyone realizes how much we are affected by new developments and if the computer age has taught us anything, it is that we must adjust in order to keep up with the times.

Tennis is no exception. In the past twenty years there have been countless advancements in the sport. Oversized racquets, modern footwear, the grip for the groundstroke — even the style of play are all being altered and refined as the game advances. While all these changes have made their impact on the sport, perhaps nothing has changed actual play as much as the development of an offensive groundstroke weapon.

The offensive weapon we're referring to is nothing more than a combination of a forehand groundstroke with court strategy to force errors and make openings for an attack to finish the point. For a long time, classical court strategy was to never run around your backhand unless the ball was in the center of the court. Even today, many players use the same style. They hit balls crosscourt concentrating the majority of the shots in the general vicinity of the opponent's backhand.

(NOTE: Even as they do this, most players forget depth and only worry about direction.)

When the opponent returns the shot, these same players will usually hit a forehand or backhand depending on which side of the court the ball comes to. Far too often, the only time a player will move around to hit a forehand is if the ball is hit directly down the middle. After

Classical Approach

this shot, the player will follow the classic style and immediately recover to the middle of the court.

But things have changed. This style of play is outdated and players who want to stay with the times will have to follow a new strategy: Hit deep balls to your opponent's weaker stroke. Throw in some high floaters and occasionally hit a few drop shots. Then when your opponent hits a weak or short return **run around** your backhand and hit **a big offensive forehand.**

Runaround Forehand

After this offensive shot, your opponent's return, if he gets it, will be defensive and shallow. Be ready to move to the net to finish off the point. With this strategy you're taking the offensive. You're attacking when your opponent has given you an opening. Nobody uses this style of play better than Borg, Lendl or Wilander. They have changed with the times and, since it involves nothing more than practice, you should follow along.

There are five elements of this strategy to remember:
1. Your deep groundstrokes set up the short balls.
2. Keep your opponent off balance with your shot selections.
3. When you get the short ball, hit an offensive shot.
4. Don't expect the forcing shot to be a clean winner so be ready to finish the point off with a volley.
5. This is the total game of consistent groundstrokes setting up the weak return and using a forehand weapon to win.

The Lesson

Nick — *Jimmy, today I want to practice hitting forehands and backhands, concentrating on being consistent and accurate. I'll put three to five targets three feet inside the baseline — one in each corner and one in the middle. That will help you position your shots. Remember, do everything the same as in all your shots:*

1. *Watch the ball.*
2. *Prepare quickly, taking the racquet head back fast once you determine which stoke you'll hit.*
3. *Get your racquet head below the ball on the forehand part of the stroke.*
4. *Hit through the ball with a big follow-through and keep your wrist firm on contact.*
5. *Keep your feet moving to get into position.*

You're doing well today Jimmy, but don't take chances from deep in your backcourt. Trying to hit too close to the lines will only lose points from that part of the court. And get under the ball. Lift it up higher over the net.

Jimmy — *Nick, I notice when I hit the ball real deep to you, some of your returns occasionally come back very shallow.*

Nick — *You're right. My shallow returns are a direct result of your deep groundstrokes. Now let's do something more with the ball when I hit a short one to you. Since you're most confident with your forehand, we'll develop it into an offensive weapon. I'll feed you balls about ten feet inside your baseline. They won't be hit hard, but no matter where they are I want you to hit your forehand.*

Jimmy — *Do you want me to run around my backhand and hit all my forehands for winners?*

Nick — *No, you won't be able to hit all these shots for winners. But remember, when you run around your backhand you're leaving a lot of open court. So your shot has to be offensive and well-placed. The part of the court you're in will help determine if you go for an outright winner or not.*

Probably your shot should go to one of the corners which your opponent's position will determine. Since this is an offensive shot, your opponent's return will be defensive and should be shallow. At this point your opponent is trying to recover. You should approach the net and finish off the point.

Jimmy — *Nick, we've hit about 50 balls so far, but I'm still not confident running around and hitting my forehand. It feels like I'm leaving too much open court.*

Nick — *That's a natural reaction, Jimmy. You're trying something new. Remember practice will make it better. Let's hit another hundred balls, only hit them a little harder and deeper than the last ones. Hit all forehands. (Practice drill.) Remember you have got to* **move your feet quickly** *to take advantage of that short ball. To hit with confidence you have to take the offensive attack and make sure to hit the ball above waist level if possible. Get into position every time — this is an offensive shot. This time, after you hit your shot, move to the net to take the volley. You're really looking more confident now. You're hitting the ball at waist level or above, and hitting from a low to a high position with topspin. Now you're making an offensive shot that will force your opponent into errors and weak returns. You've just developed a new weapon.*

Conclusion

This strategy will add another dimension to your game but there will never be a substitute for consistent forehands and backhands along with a reliable serve. Without those two traits, it will be hard to win. Before you can develop an offensive weapon off your groundstroke, you must be able to hit consistent shots with a high percentage of accuracy.

Once you have the basic strokes perfected, adopt the new court strategy. Develop the offensive weapon which will bring your game into the modern age.

(NOTE: This does not exclude any player who feels his backhand is far superior and wants to attack from that side.)

*Player Runs Around Short Ball
to Hit Offensive Forehand*

6

THE BACKHAND

How to Improve a One-Handed Backhand

Many players have a fear of the backhand, often developed early in their playing career. The reasons vary: lack of strength, poor footwork, or just learning the stroke after they developed a forehand.

Whatever the reason, the negative stigma that surrounds the backhand should be eliminated by the student and pro at the first chance. I teach all parts of the game together so no importance is given to any one stroke.

Remember, the backhand is a natural motion with the swing moving away from the body. Couple that with a proper grip, early preparation and positive attitude, and no one need fear the backhand. Anyone who replaces that defensive backhand with a solid groundstroke will move up another plateau.

To improve a one-handed backhand remember:
1. No less than an Eastern Backhand grip.
2. Decide quickly if you're going to hit a backhand.
3. Turn your shoulder to get the racquet back farther.
4. A fixed wrist on the backhand is essential.
5. Always follow through — don't stop your backhand swing.

The Backhand

*One-Handed
Backhand Backswing*

*One-Handed
Backhand Follow-Through*

The Lesson

Nick — *Danielle, we are going to concentrate on groundstrokes today with a little more hitting to your backhand side.*

Dani — *Is there something wrong with my backhand?*

Nick — *No, you have developed a good solid backhand, but there are a few simple suggestions that I feel will make it better. I never change anyone, but instead try to make small adjustments.*

Dani — *I feel the ball gets behind me when having to run for wide backhands.*

Nick — *To offset this trouble area, try watching the ball the second it leaves the opponent's racquet and determine whether it is going to be a forehand or backhand before it passes the net. If a backhand, turn your shoulder when taking the first step to that side. The simple shoulder turn will get your racquet head back. When arriving at the ball, you only have to start your forward motion enabling you to meet it in front.*

I also notice you are off balance when reaching the ball. Instead of stepping parallel to the ball and jamming yourself, step toward the net. This enables your weight to be going toward the position the ball is to go. You will feel as though more power has been added to your stroke and at the same time your arm and shoulder will open up with no difficulty.

I see something else that is causing you trouble with your backhand. You have a double backswing. Look at this backswing. I take the racquet head back and just before the ball arrives I pull it back a little farther. That's a double backswing. You must take it back in one motion and then forward. I am sure this will eliminate those late hits.

Dani — *You keep saying how important the backswing is. Is mine O.K.?*

Nick — *Yes, your left hand pulls the racquet head straight back with your arm fairly close to your body. Students seem to have more success with a straight back swing, but even a straight back has a slight loop to it, especially when the downswing begins. Do not concern yourself with which is better. If your present way feels natural, stay with it.*

Dani — *I also seem to overrun a lot of my balls.*

Nick — *I suggest you begin to reach a little more for the ball. It is easier to make an adjustment forward than to back away at the last minute. One more suggestion. The backhand swing is away from your body which means you can always follow through no matter what. Too many people stop their swing if they are not in perfect position. I am going to hit a few balls right at you and prove you can follow through no matter what. Hit it. Don't stop your follow-through! That's still not good enough. Finish the swing no matter what. Don't worry about what it looks like as long as the ball goes over the net. They don't judge you on looks but on who keeps the ball in play the longest. Watch Harold Solomon. He is never on the ground, has very unorthodox strokes but he wins because he keeps the ball going. Winners are not determined by looks!*

It is also important to maintain a firm wrist on contact and hit through the ball trying to hold it on your racquet as long as possible. If you hesitate when making contact or just before, control of the ball will be lost! A great many errors occur if you do not keep a firm wrist on contact. By collapsing the wrist you'll lose control.

Dani — *I want to get more power on my backhand. Should I switch to two hands?*

Nick — *It is not necessary to go to two hands for power. Try this: Turn your shoulder a little more. This will get the racquet back a little farther. This additional backswing made by a little more shoulder rotation will give extra power.*

Dani — *Why can't I pull my racquet head back more or lay my wrist back for power rather than a shoulder turn?*

Nick — *A fixed wrist position on the backswing is essential. This position along with an Eastern Backhand grip that you use requires very little wrist adjustment when making contact.*

Dani — *Some of my friends have Continental grips and say it is easier because they do not have to change at all for either backhand and forehand, and this helps when hard balls are hit to them.*

Nick — *The Continental grip places the "V" more on top of the racquet which for most people means loss of strength. Unless you have a wrist like Rod Laver or Lew Hoad, I suggest you use the Eastern Backhand grip. The majority of players change their grips and so can you, if you prepare quickly and anticipate to what side the ball is coming before it crosses the net. The Eastern Backhand requires very little wrist adjustment to get the racquet head perpendicular when meeting the ball. Anyone can improve his backhand with a few simple adjustments. Just remember this: Relax and let the racquet head do the work for you.*

Conclusion

Perhaps no other shot causes such unnecessary concern and worry as the backhand. To improve the stroke, most players have only to improve their own self-confidence. To do it, practice quickness. Watch the ball as your opponent swings and try to determine whether the return will force you to hit a forehand or a backhand before the ball crosses the net.

Once you decide, get into position quickly, keep your wrist firm, turn your shoulder to get the racquet back and follow through. Don't worry about appearance. Let your racquet head provide the momentum to carry the ball across the net. Getting into position quickly and hitting with confidence are the two best ways of improving a weak backhand stroke.

Topspin Backhand

The topspin backhand is an important shot for players to have in their repertoire because opponents often attack backhands and topspin allows you to hit the ball hard and still keep it in the court. Topspin makes the ball bounce quite high and thus it is difficult for your opponent to handle from deep in the court. The topspin backhand is also quite useful against opponents who either serve and volley or attack the net — the topspin causes the ball to dip very quickly and the balls are difficult to volley.

Achieving topspin on the backhand is not much different than generating the spin on the forehand side. The racquet head starts below the ball and a brushing motion is used on the forward part of the swing with a high follow-through. For this type of backhand, I advise the player to maintain a firm wrist throughout the stroke, and use an Eastern Backhand or a more exaggerated backhand grip.

Players may feel they do not achieve as much topspin on their backhand as they do on their forehands. This is only natural since most players feel physically stronger on their forehand side. However, the topspin you get when hitting from a low to a high with the proper grip is usually sufficient to keep you in the game.

These are important elements to the topspin backhand:

1. If using an Eastern Backhand grip and you want more topspin, then exaggerate the grip. NOTE: Change your grip only if you're willing to spend a lot of time practicing.
2. Regular backswing.
3. Get the racquet head below the ball.
4. Brush the ball from a low to a high.
5. Have a high follow-through.
6. Maintain a firm wrist throughout the stroke.

The Backhand

Topspin Backhand

The Lesson

Nick — *Jimmy, I feel we can develop more topspin by preparing earlier and lowering the racquet head under the ball on the forward part of the swing.*

Jimmy — *I want you to help me because it's really important to get more topspin. The professional tour is far different from the junior ranks. The players serve and volley, attack on short balls and even come in on my second serve.*

Nick — *Well, then, let's work on it. You seem to be hesitant when making contact with the ball and you stop right after contact. You must accelerate the racquet head with an upward motion, exaggerate the follow-through and be very relaxed throughout the entire stroke.*

Jimmy — *I have been watching a lot of the players in their warmups and practice. When playing Lendl, I noticed a different grip for his heavy topspin backhand.*

Nick — *Several of the players seem to be using the same grip including Clerc, Vilas, Gunthardt and, of course, Lendl. It is a Semi-Western Hammer grip backhand. I am very hesitant for you to use the Hammer grip with fingers close together, but I feel a little turn to the left of your Eastern Backhand grip will offer you the same spin. A week before the Pro Indoors I changed Chip Hooper to that grip and the results were very positive. I also suggested he hit low underspins and chips to Connors' backhand side. This required Chip to revert to his Eastern Backhand grip. For your underspins you should do the same.*

Jimmy — *Should I hit everything with this grip?*

Nick — *Absolutely not. Because of the position of your wrist with the Semi-Western grip, it is difficult to hit low balls and just as hard to hit effective underspin or touch shots.*

Jimmy — *When I first started playing, my Dad told me how important it was to hit from a low to a high, to have an Eastern Backhand grip and finish with a very high follow-through with a firm wrist on contact and to be relaxed at all times.*

Nick — *If everyone followed that advice, all backhands would have topspin. Of course, only those who can practice several hours each day should attempt heavy topspin from the backhand side.*

Conclusion

In order to stay with the opposition, you will have to have some knowledge of topspin backhand. However, unless you're playing very stiff competition, you will not need more topspin than you get from simply hitting from a low to a high with a quick brushing motion. Keep your wrist firm during the stroke and do not lead with your elbow — it may cause long-term physical damage.

The Underspin Backhand

The underspin or slice backhand has many uses and should be learned. It can be used offensively, defensively or as an approach shot. The underspin backhand gives a player the opportunity to change pace. It adds control and provides variety that is helpful in keeping your opponent off balance. If hit correctly, the underspin backhand will bounce very low. The low bounce proves invaluable when hitting approach shots or when trying to throw off a two-handed player's backhand.

The underspin backhand requires very little energy to execute. On the forward part of the swing, you must hit down and out with the follow-through slightly up at the end. Brushing the back of the ball gives it underspin. If you first make contact with the bottom of the ball, too much underspin will be applied and these shots will cross the net with a high trajectory or be ineffective because of a high bounce.

The underspin backhand is not part of my first lesson in teaching groundstrokes. However, I feel it must be learned by my students if they are to develop into all-around players.

The following are important points about this shot:
1. Underspin is a very effective shot which can be offensive or defensive.
2. Most people lose complete control when hitting this shot too hard.
3. The underspin is excellent in changing the pace of the game. It gives you time to regain center position and recover from your opponent's offensive stroke.

The Lesson

Nick — *Jimmy, your backhand is very solid, but today let's add the underspin backhand to your arsenal. It will only require a small adjustment.*

Jimmy — *Isn't the underspin backhand a defensive stroke?*

Nick — *Yes, and no, even though hit defensively and with less power, it can do several positive offensive things for you which are needed if you are to develop into an all-around player.*

Jimmy — *Why didn't you start me with the underspin backhand?*

Nick — *After working with so many students, I found that teaching the pure offensive strokes first produces the best results.*

Jimmy — *Tell me some of the good points of the underspin backhand.*

Nick — *Your underspin could throw off your opponent's rhythm, especially when you groove the stroke so that it can be hit aggressively without sacrificing consistency and accuracy. This shot, because of the underspin, will allow you more time to close into the net to get set for a volley. In addition, the spin gives you control and a low bouncing ball which makes it difficult for your opponent to hit a clean passing shot.*

Jimmy — *Do I have to change my backswing, face of the racquet or use my wrist to develop this shot? I remember watching Ken Rosewall. It looked like his racquet face was parallel to the ground on contact with the ball. I also saw Lutz stand on his toes when hitting his underspin. His racquet face also looked parallel to the ground.*

Nick — *It may look as though the face is open, but if it were, and the shot was hit fairly hard, the ball would sail out. The face of the racquet may be open before contact, but the racquet heads of both Rosewall and Lutz are just about vertical with the first contact with the ball. After the first contact, they continue down the lower backside of the ball finishing the stroke out and slightly up. By the way, they maintain a firm wrist at all times.*

I suggest you keep your racquet face the same for all of your shots — slightly open. If you change your backswing at any time to hit certain shots, the opponent will begin to read your stroke and you will lose the element of surprise. It really is important to be able to hit all of your shots with consistency and accuracy. Do not attempt to be a master of everything, but only those strokes which are essential to an all-around game.

Conclusion

Many people have a tendency to hit down on the ball and then stop their follow-through on contact. Instead, try hitting down and through and keep the racquet head on the ball a little longer. When the stroke is finished, the racquet head should be slightly above the point where you initially made contact.

Remember, the underspin backhand requires little energy, but used correctly, can improve your position as much as any power shot.

Is the Two-Handed Backhand for You?

Every day I work with a wide variety of students. They range in age from youngsters to seniors and in skill levels from highly ranked to novice. But no matter what level of play, one of the most frequently asked questions is whether or not to use a two-handed backhand.

My answer depends upon each individual taking into account strength, mobility, coordination and time devoted to play. Both methods are fine. Both have advantages and disadvantages. In all honesty, I hesitate to tell anyone which style to adopt. It's a question each individual should answer for himself. When a student is in doubt, I watch him hit both styles during a lesson then decide based on which method seems more suited to his style of play.

The greatest advantage of the two-handed backhand is the added power it gives a shot. Many players use the two-handed method because they needed the extra strength when they were young and as they matured, they refined their techniques according to their style.

Tracy Austin, Chris Evert Lloyd, Jimmy Connors and Bjorn Borg have all spent countless hours refining their techniques with two hands. They have taken advantage of the assets of the two hands — power, reliability, disguise, heavy topspin — and become the success stories of that method.

For the one-handed backhand, the biggest advantage is reach. To be effective using two hands, one must be able to move to position faster and, once reaching the ball, the player must have a more closed stance to hit it. The two-handed player must work harder to reach low balls and must have adequate speed to reach high floating balls that back them up.

Another advantage of a one-handed backhand is the ability to return serves hit directly at them. A good strategy when playing someone using two-handed returns is to serve directly at them. Jamming is often successful.

As if there wasn't enough confusion about this decision, there are actually two different styles of two-handed backhands: the guide backhand and the wrap-around backhand. The guide backhand uses both the arms and racquet together with elbow extension far away from the body. The racquet and arms point to the position they want the ball to go.

The long extension of the arms is the key factor to the depth and

Two-Handed Backhand for You

Two-Handed Backhand with Guide Follow-Through and Wrap Follow-Through

power generated with this style. The best examples are Chris Evert Lloyd and Tracy Austin. Both use this style of backhand to pin opponents to the baseline.

For pure acceleration, the wrap-around style can't be beat. With this method the arms bend on contact and come up and over your right shoulder. This stroke produces a great deal of topspin but requires precision timing. Mis-hits are common with this style. Andrea Jeager follows the wrap-around backhand but uses less wrist acceleration than Borg.

To master the wrap-around you must be willing to dedicate many hours to practice. If you don't spend time with it, you'll have trouble developing depth, consistency or accuracy.

Put in the practice time and you may hit them like the master of the wrap-around, Borg, who uses his topspin backhand to set up the rest of his balanced attack.

Again, both styles have advantages and disadvantages. Personally I recommend the two-handed guide method for my students because it is easier to master. However, if you feel capable of hitting the wrap-around, go to it. Both methods are useful. They are excellent for baseline rallies and they work effectively against net rushers and for return of serve.

Once a decision is made to switch to a two-handed backhand, the next question is grip. Again, I try to suggest a style which is most natural and comfortable for the student, though generally I suggest one of two grips — both of which have proven successful.

The first has both hands in an Eastern Forehand grip. This grip provides equal strength from both hands and allows the student to guide the ball throughout the stroke.

Two-Handed Backhand using Two Eastern Forehand Grips

Another successful grip has a combination approach. In this grip the bottom hand is in a Continental grip and the top hand in an Eastern Forehand grip. This grip is somewhat more versatile than the double Eastern Forehand style. The combination allows the student to let go and follow through with one hand on wide and short balls and on volleys at the net.

Two-Handed Backhand with Bottom Hand in Continental Grip

There are, of course, other grips for two-handed shots, but the grips I suggest work for most of my students. If you use something different — and it works for you — stick with it.

Since many people are interested in the two-handed backhand, and since I recommend the guide backhand, I will follow with a sample lesson that may help you evaluate whether to go to this method.

Guided Backhand Lesson

Pearson — *Nick, my backhand is not reliable. My wrist feels like spaghetti, especially when hard balls are hit to me or when I'm returning serves.*

Nick — *I think we can work on that problem. Throughout our lesson today I will attack your backhand whenever possible and we'll evaluate the difficulties. The first thing I want you to do is to get your racquet back as soon as you know you're going to hit a backhand. That should eliminate most of the errors. Get to the ball and hit with more confidence.*

I see you're still having trouble. Your backhand looks weak. Slide your left hand down the throat of your racquet until it is above your right hand. Now try hitting with two hands.

Pearson — *Do I have to hold it a certain way?*

Nick — *For the first few balls just hit with your same forehand grip and hold your left hand where it is comfortable. Just believe you're hitting a two-handed forehand. Relax and let the racquet do the work for you.*

You're doing fine. You're using an Eastern Forehand grip with both hands and it's working. Now take the racquet back at waist height with your arms a little closer to your body. Don't rush the forward part of your swing. Relax and let your arms get away from your body just a little more. Very good. Just guide the ball. With this method, you don't use your wrists. Stay with the ball longer. Do not go around your shoulder on the follow-through. Let your arms extend toward me. It might seem a little awkward at first — especially when you have to reach for low balls or when you run wide — but most people have the same initial sensation. In order to overcome that awkwardness you must move your feet quicker and make position faster to offset the feeling.

You're doing much better. You can also hit topspins the very same way you do it on your forehand. Get the racquet head below the ball and hit from a low to a high with a sharp brushing motion.

Conclusion

Only you should determine whether to use a two-handed backhand or not — and if you decide to use it, you should use the grip which seems most natural.

On the plus side, two-handed backhands are usually quite steady and reliable. But two-handed players can be jammed on serves and balls hit directly at them. They also lack range and reach.

Perhaps the most important element of backhands has nothing to do with how many hands you're using. If you're having trouble with backhands, don't change anything until you are sure you're getting your racquet back quickly. The moment you decide you're going to hit a backhand, get your racquet back in position. This should eliminate most backhand problems.

Two-Handed Backhand — One-Hand Release

There are definite times when the one-hand or the two-handed backhand has an advantage over the other. Where one style allows greater reach, the other offers more power. It is impossible for me to say where and when not to release your left hand, although I agree with Cliff Drysdale when he says a great many two-handed players should release one hand occasionally — especially on the volley.

You, the individual, should determine your limitations and capabilities and decide if you should release one hand — or even if you should switch entirely to a one-handed backhand style. However, no matter what you decide, I suggest you start releasing your left hand in practice every day to get the feeling and confidence to do it in a match because no matter how good your two-handed style is, there will be times when it's impossible to reach certain shots.

Two-Handed Backhand with One-Hand Release

The following are thoughts to consider about the two-handed backhand — one-hand release:

1. Strength is added to your weaker side. Physically, young juniors and even adults do not have the strength to pull the racquet forward in contrast to the forehand where the hand pushes the racquet. The left hand gives this extra strength helping guide the racquet to the contact point. It's even more important if the ball gets behind the hitter.

2. The grip for the right hand, at a minimum, should be an Eastern Forehand, but I suggest my students have a Continental which gives strength when reaching for wide balls and in volleys when the left hand is released.

3. For some people it is not natural to hit with two hands but they cannot control the racquet with one.

4. There are advanced strokes that are difficult to perform with

a total two-hand shot, such as the drop shot, return of high
balls, especially high bouncing serves and short low bouncing balls.

5.   To be a total two-handed player requires more natural ability and coordination, especially when having to run for the
wide ball.

The Lesson

Nick — *Throughout our baseline rallies, Louis, I am going to move
you around the court and try several wide backhands, some
drop shots and high balls deep to your backhand.*

Louis — *I notice that when you hit short angle, wide low balls to
my backhand, I have trouble doing very much with the ball.*

Nick — *Unless you are exceptionally fast on your feet, you will have
trouble. Everyone does — because of limited reach when
going to the ball. You may feel awkward and off balance.
A few times I even noticed you let go with your left hand.
The ball went over but too high and out. It is not wrong
to release the left hand. The reason the ball went high and
out is because of your grip with the right hand. The Semi-
Western to Eastern Forehand grip has your hand behind
the handle. When hitting a one-hand backhand with this
grip, the face of the racquet will open on contact, giving
you very little control of the ball. Move your hand to the
Continental grip. Then you can hit the two-handed
backhand with a one-hand release. That's right. And it also
makes it possible to volley from both sides when coming
to the net with no other grip adjustments.*

Louis — *Now that I'm getting stronger, I really would like to hit
more one-handed backhands. Two-handed backhands have
never felt natural or comfortable to me.*

Nick — *Let's hit the next balls with two hands using your new grip
and after contact release the left hand. Don't let go too soon.
Hold on to it a little longer with your left hand. With time,
after practicing the one-hand release, we can determine
whether or not to be a complete one-hand backhand.*

Louis — *Let's do it right now!*

Nick — *I feel a* **major** *change should come about in stages. Having
the help of the left hand, especially on service returns and
net rushes, allows you to place more topspin because of added strength.*

Louis — *I still have trouble trying to hit drop shots, underslices and high bouncing balls with the two-handed backhand.*

Nick — *It is more natural to hit those shots with one hand. The reason you have difficulty with them is because of your original Semi-Western-Eastern Forehand grip. This grip makes it difficult to adjust your wrist and tilt of the racquet to get under the ball for the drop shot and underslice. It is more difficult to hold the ball on the racquet with two hands. High bouncing balls are really tough to reach with two hands. You should hit those shots with a long, one-handed follow-through.*

Louis — *Gene Mayer and Jimmy Connors hold on with two hands almost all the time, and no one hits better touch shots than Gene.*

Nick — *You are correct, but they are excellent athletes who hit thousands of balls each day. Do not judge your game by anyone else's standards. Within the next few weeks, your results will tell us if we should make additional adjustments to your backhand.*

Conclusion

No one can tell you whether it is better to use the two-handed backhand entirely — or to release with one hand. However, there are times when, for no other reason than reach, you will have to go to one hand. For this reason, I suggest you make a habit of practicing the one-hand release.

For those who use the two-handed backhand, a one-hand release should help you hit drop shots, underslices and high bouncing balls. Practice the one-handed release on those shots so you'll be comfortable during matches.

7

THE VOLLEY

Forehand and Backhand

The volley is simply a shot that is hit before the ball bounces. A player usually hits the volley inside the service line, however, volleys can be hit from any area in the court.

There are many different types of volleys as well as different places from which to hit them. The different types of volleys are the quick exchange (reflex), first or approach volley and the put-away volley. Volleys are usually hit from near the service line to the net; volleys hit deep in the court are usually for advanced players playing an aggressive game.

Some players fear volleying, often because they learned the volley late in their game. Learning the volley late often puts a stigma of difficulty or risk on the shot. This is a fear players cannot afford to have. Practice will help overcome this hesitation.

The best time to learn the volley is early in a player's development. When teaching the beginner a volley, there are certain guidelines to be followed. These guidelines are not rigid because most players develop certain styles that work well for them. However, a question which is repeatedly asked is which grip should be used for the volley? My answer requires an explanation.

Each grip has positive and negative points about it. The Continental grip offers a player the same grip for both forehand and backhand volleys. This is a great asset because with no change of grip all the player must do is hit the ball. The disadvantage is a loss of strength, especially when the ball is behind the volleyer. The Eastern Forehand and Backhand grip can also be used on the volley. The disadvantage of changing grips is made up for by added strength. Each player should be the judge as to which grip or grips are best.

Remember, learn the volley early and use good fundamentals and you will hit volleys with accuracy and confidence.

The following are some important suggestions to remember about the basic volley:

1. Get into a good ready position. Be alert at all times, like a goaltender or shortstop watching the puck or baseball.
2. Get your feet spread shoulder width apart. Relax your knees. Hold your racquet directly in front of you with your elbows away from the body. Make sure your left hand holds the throat of the racquet. That hand will help a great deal in changing your grip.
3. You must watch the ball leave your opponent's racquet and try to meet it in front of you.
4. Do nothing but block the ball. Actually try to catch it without throwing it back.

The Lesson

Nick — *Geoffrey, come up to the net. I want to speak to you.*

Geoffrey — *Why are you hitting balls right at me when you said to come up to talk to you?*

Nick — *To show you a new shot. You just hit a forehand volley.*

Geoffrey — *All I did was block the ball.*

Nick — *Why didn't you swing at it as you do with your groundstrokes?*

Geoffrey — *I didn't have time. The ball was at me before I knew it and the only way to block it was by holding my racquet up.*

Nick — *That was your first volley. Blocking the ball! To be a good volleyer you must be alert at all times. Watch the ball leave the opponent's racquet to determine whether it is a forehand or backhand and immediately prepare to block it from that side with a firm wrist.*

Geoffrey — *What grip should I use?*

Nick — *For our first few lessons use the same Eastern Forehand and Eastern Backhand grip you use on your forehand and backhand groundstrokes.*

Forehand Volley

Backhand Volley

Geoffrey — *I like that. Some of the kids said they had to learn one grip (Continental) for their volleys.*

Nick — *What did they think about that?*

Geoffrey — *They all had different opinions. Some of the younger juniors liked changing their grip because they felt very weak with the Continental grip. Others felt it took too much time!*

Nick — *Well, both opinions are correct. Everyone should use whichever grip feels best. You're hitting the volley better, now let's try the backhand side.*

Geoffrey — *That's not fair. You said it was coming to my backhand so I changed my grip and you hit it to my forehand, I didn't have time to change my grip.*

Nick — *You will find that very same thing happening again. You must be more alert to allow time to change your grip or you must use the same grip for all your volleys.*

Geoffrey — *Let's try it.*

Nick — *I will feed one ball at a time going back and forth to forehand and backhand. Ready? That's good, try turning your shoulder a little more. Use your left hand to hold the throat of the racquet especially when on the backhand side. It will give you more strength with the same grip.*

Geoffrey — *That feels good, but I just don't feel strong.*

Nick — *In time, you will get stronger. Meeting the ball in front will make up for the loss of strength. Let's continue.*

Geoffrey — *Why do so many of my balls go into the net?*

Nick — *When you make contact with the ball, you go down. It is important to keep the racquet head on the same height as the ball and go through it, not down.*

Geoffrey — *My balls still go all over the place.*

Nick — *A firm wrist on contact should eliminate that problem.*

Geoffrey — *Do I ever use my wrist?*

Nick — *At this stage it is best to keep your wrist firm with little or no layback. Also you open the face of the racquet too much. This can be eliminated by your elbows being away from your body in the ready position and when making contact with the ball. There will be times when you must open the face of the racquet, especially on low balls and for first volleys in the service area. Underspin will offset the open face, adding control to the ball.*

Geoffrey — *I hit so many of my volleys off-center.*

Nick — *It is extremely important to watch the ball every second. Do not think of anything but making contact with the ball in front of you.*

Geoffrey — *Can I put more power on my volleys?*

Nick — *It is important to keep the volley in play. Power and placement will develop with confidence, practice, patience and sound fundamentals. These are the keys to success in this stage of your volley. As you gain confidence with your volleys, timing and anticipation will allow you to start doing a little more with your shots.*

Geoffrey — *Does that mean I can start swinging at my volleys like John Newcombe?*

Nick — *There are very few players who can execute a swinging volley like John Newcombe but experienced volleyers will take a little swing and follow-through on some of their volleys, especially sitting ducks.*

Geoffrey — *What is a sitting duck?*

Nick — *It happens quite often if your approach shot or overhead places the opponent in a complete defensive position. He will attempt to get the ball back, but it has no power, or depth, and sits up fairly close to the net. On this shot you can add a little more swing to your stroke. Position will determine what you can and should do with your volleys.*

Conclusion

Volleys are important to anyone's game and should be learned as soon as possible. The shot need not be anything more than a blocking motion hit in front of you. The correct grip is a question only you can answer, but keep your wrist firm on contact and be alert. This shot often takes quick reflexes, so watch the ball as it leaves your opponent's racquet.

First Volley

The first volley is probably the single most important stroke for players who serve and volley, or for those players who come in on controlled approach shots. A player unable to hit a deep controlled first volley from the area of the service line loses the offensive.

The first volley from the service line area must be well-placed and deep or the attacker will be on the defense. With a good first volley the returner will be forced to hit a defensive return. Now the ball can be put away with a simple punch volley.

Remember, when practicing the first volley, depth and placement are the two key elements.

The following are important points about the first volley:

1. Meet the ball far out in front of you. This will eliminate a great deal of your backswing.
2. Slow down and come to a stop in order to control your body movement.
3. Have a slight shoulder turn and step toward the net with your left foot for the forehand volley.
4. Maintain a firm wrist and go through the ball with a slight follow-through.
5. The first volley is a placement shot, not a winner.

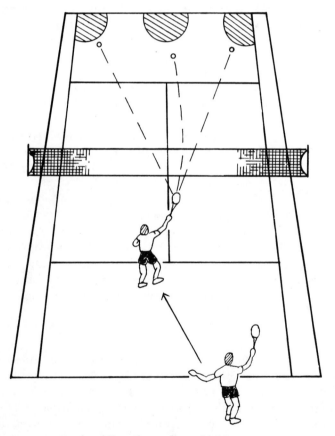

Place first volleys deep

The Lesson

Nick — *Let's keep score in our lesson today. You must serve and volley.*

Louis — *You were lucky to win that point.*

Nick — *Perhaps, but you hit a very poor first volley. You ran through the volley! Stan Smith often said the key to the volley is coming to a complete stop as your opponent hits the ball. This stop gives you body control to move in any direction for the first volley. 0-15.*

Louis — *Look at that. Another good serve and volley and still you passed me.*

Nick — *The object of the first volley is position and depth, making it difficult for me to hit an offensive shot. Your volley landed on the service line. 0-30.*

Louis — *That will never happen again. You ready?*

Nick — *0-40. You went from a defensive first volley to an outright winner. This is a low percentage shot unless you are capable of moving in very close to the net very much like Vitas Gerulaitis.*

Louis — *15-40. I really concentrated on the ball and thought of the target area we worked on.*

Nick — *You must really dig in to pull yourself out of a hole. Serve again, Louis.*

Louis — *Just one more question. I feel like going for more direct winners and even trying some short angle volleys.*

Nick — *Try to think of yourself as a gambler and you always want the odds in your favor. Your first volley should be hit to the portion of the court that you are able to see above the net. Anything less than this means trouble. To see more of the court, learn to close into the net sooner. If you try for a winner, you join the "elite group" making too many unforced errors. Pay heed to my advice and do not take needless risks.*

Louis — *30-40. You see, I hit my first volley down the line as you told me.*

Nick — *That's right. Hit the majority of your first volleys down the line. You will come out ahead.*

Louis — *I'm after you now.*

Nick — *Fault. Second service. My game! You eased up far too much on your second serve, giving me time to run around my backhand and hit my big forehand for a winner. You must apply pressure on your opponent at all times before attemp-*

Go down the line with your first volley

ting your first volley. If you don't, you will be paying for
the balls.

Louis — *Let's practice our first volleys. I feel about ready to make
the breakthrough.*

Nick — *Try positioning yourself in the vicinity of the service line.
I will stand inside the baseline three to five feet. Let's volley
back and forth to each other. Half-volleys don't count when
hit to me. This drill will force you to hit through the volleys,
gaining depth and accuracy.*

Louis — *I do fairly well on my first volleys above the net, but I fear
the low ones.*

Nick — *Learn to move in faster, but remember, there are times the
return will be extremely effective and down at your feet.
You have to get down to the level of the ball. Open your
racquet face slightly on contact. This produces underspin
when lifting it above the level of the net.*

Louis — *There are still times I just can't be offensive on my first
volleys.*

Nick — *Try volleying your first ball deep, directly down the center.
This will force your opponent to move before hitting his
passing shot. By the way, your mis-hits can be eliminated
by total concentration on the ball. Do not concern yourself
about where the opponent is going, but only on your volley.
You know where you want to place it.* **Do not change your
mind. Concentrate.** *Don't keep one eye on the ball and
the other on the opponent.*

Louis — *This is really a good lesson, but is there any specific exercise to help me cut down my backswing?*

Nick — *Come over to my side and place yourself right up to the fence. Let's volley back and forth to each other from here.*

Louis — *That's not fair. I can't take my racquet back without hitting the fence.*

Nick — **Stop! You just said the magic word: too big a swing gets you into trouble.** *Practice against the fence every day. You will develop a short and simple first volley.*

Conclusion

The speed of the ball and your court position will dictate the volley you use. Only advanced players should consider more than a short punch motion, especially on their first volley. The first volley usually determines the outcome of the point. It is imperative to place the first volley deep into your opponent's backcourt. Try to get them to hit their returns while off balance. This volley should not be an outright winner.

Do not wait for the ball to come to you. Go after it with a positive attitude and meet the ball slightly in front of you with the weight of your body going in the direction of your shot.

Be sure to use your opponent's ball speed. Do not try to generate any more than the actual speed coming at you, unless the ball is floating; and remember, a little underspin is good for control.

Shoulder Volleys (Swinging)

The volley, for the most part, is taught as a compact stroke with very little swing. However, there are times when an opponent hits a floater, a ball that just sits up in the air. For these balls, I recommend a shoulder or swinging volley. Of course, one will not master the swinging volley immediately. It will take practice to attack those floating balls with a full stroke like John Newcombe.

However, with practice you can turn the floating balls into winners and good approach shots by using the stroking volley. Never forget your short compact stroke, because for the majority of your volleys, you will still use it.

Remember, the stroking volley makes a player an offensive threat. The stroking volley, if you perfect it, may cause your opponents to go for low percentage shots when returning your balls, causing more errors for them and more points for you.

The following are important shoulder volley tips:

1.   Make sure the elbow is away from your body. Excessive wrist

Forehand Shoulder Volley

Backhand Shoulder Volley

and shoulder body movements occur when the elbow is tucked into the body. The reach is also cut down.

2. Power is generated on the volley by a shoulder turn and the forward movement of your body. Be sure to volley with your arm away from your body.

3. Be sure to practice the shoulder volley on those floating balls in practice so you'll be confident in a match.

The Lesson

Nick — *Pam, I feel you are not doing enough with your high volleys, especially inside the service line area.*

Pam — *I don't know what you mean. My shot is a short punch motion, and I try to place it deep into your backcourt so I can move in for the put-away.*

Nick — *That is exactly right. I do not want you to change that tactic, especially if the return is a hard drive or return of service. But let's add the swinging shoulder volley to your game for those balls you have time to swing at.*

Pam — *I will do my best.*

Nick — *That's still a block volley. Take your racquet head back a little more and swing through the ball. Do not swing down. Let the racquet head stay on the same level of the ball. Better, much better. Do not worry if some of your shots go out in the beginning.*

Pam — *It's starting to feel more natural to me, but at times my balance is not the greatest.*

Nick — *You have great feet! That is what it takes for this shot. You can correct the balance problem by turning and stepping with that left foot. This gets the shoulder turn, which adds more power to your shot. This turn prepares you to close into the net for the short put-away.*

Pam — *That's what concerns me. If I take a full stroke and the ball does come back, I won't have time to respond.*

Nick — *The swinging volley should produce a defensive return giving you time for the next shot.*

Conclusion

When you try the shoulder volley, you can't do better than to follow the example of John Newcombe. I will try to point out why he was so successful.

He moved into the net with very fast quick steps. His preparation was excellent with a very firm wrist at all times. On low volleys he applied a firm wrist, short swing and stayed with the ball.

I do not recommend this volley to the average player unless he is prepared to practice it daily — and that means hundreds and hundreds of times. It requires many thousands of practice swings to develop a new habit.

Quick-Exchange Volley

Advancement through the ranks will require adjustments to your existing strokes. The first stage of the volley is nothing more than an infrequent visit to the net, a simple block volley and a quick retreat to the baseline.

Doubles indirectly forces you to spend more time at the net; the result: quicker volley exchanges. Unless an adjustment is made to your volley, winning points will be a rarity.

To win your share of points you will need an adjustment to your volley: a shorter backswing. At the net, quickness and concentration are essential.

The following are important elements to remember about the quick-exchange volley:

1.   An excellent ready position.
2.   Keep your wrist firm.
3.   You must keep total concentration.
4.   Do not take a big backswing.
5.   Don't stand up straight.
6.   Do nothing more than block the ball.

The Lesson

Nick — *Brian, help me out with my lesson today. Volley the balls back to my student, but try to position the shots to require some movement.*

Brian — *I'll try.*

Nick — *Brian, get your racquet up. Concentrate on the ball.*

Brian — *Gosh, I never thought it was this difficult to volley.*

Nick — *Let me show you a few drills and tips that will really help. To volley effectively in quick exchanges requires total concentration, good ready position, a short backswing and a firm wrist. You are taking too big a backswing. Because of this, it's almost impossible to meet the ball in front of you when it's hit at a high rate of speed. Let's go back to the backcourt area and play a game.*

Brian — *You want me to stand so close to the fence that my backside is just about touching?*

Nick — *That's right.*

With back to fence work on improving Quick Exchange Volley

Brian — *I feel awkward in this position.*

Nick — *That's not unusual when learning a new technique. I am going to stand on the baseline and volley back and forth with you. Ready?*

Brian — *This is tough. My racquet keeps hitting the fence, especially on the forehand side.*

Nick — *Too big a backswing. Don't stand up so straight. Get your racquet far in front of you and do nothing more than block my ball. Good, much better.*

Brian — *It feels better, but I still can't control the ball.*

Nick — *Maintain a firm wrist at all times. Now move into your normal volleying position on the court.*

Brian — *I can't believe the difference in just a few minutes. Standing this close to the net in quick exchange volleys reminds me of one important point. Short backswing or hit fence!*

Nick — *By daily practice, I sincerely feel you will become a great volleyer.*

Conclusion

Not only do you have to volley the ball quickly, but you must concentrate on placement as well. This exercise will eventually help your quick-exchange volley. When you practice this shot, have your partner stand far inside the service line. The key to this quick-exchange volley is a good ready position, short backswing and firm wrist!

Brian Gottfried, a former student of mine, was voted one of the top volleyers in the world. Quoting Brian from "Tennis Magazine": "I learned to volley by being a backboard for Nick during his lessons for several years."

The Half-Volley — Half a Groundstroke

The half-volley is not really a volley. However, it contains many similarities such as the short backswing, firm wrist and a shorter follow-through than a normal groundstroke.

The half-volley is used when you have to pick up the ball on the bounce when it is low to your feet. This shot is used when your opponent has hit a good return of serve and you are unable to volley. The same is true for someone coming in too slowly on an approach shot. You use the half-volleys only on those shots.

If you find yourself constantly hitting half-volleys in singles and even in doubles something is wrong! Try to volley the ball whenever possible.

Remember the half-volley is really "half-groundstroke and half-volley." Avoid the shot if you can, but hit with confidence when you have to.

Forehand Half-Volley   *Backhand Half-Volley*

The following are important elements of the half-volley:
1. You must not hit the ball on the run. Slow down and concentrate on the ball only.
2. When lifting the ball, try to hit down the line and as deep as possible. This will allow you time to get to the net.
3. Get down to the ball.
4. Do not jerk, jump or use body motion. Try to meet the ball with confidence and a very fluent smooth motion, letting the racquet head and firm wrist do the work.

<h3 style="text-align:center">The Lesson</h3>

Nick — *Charles, I watched your match yesterday and noticed the difficulties you had with balls. You tried to hit the ball on the rise.*

Charles — *You're right. I had trouble with them.*

Nick — *There is a simple solution. You are taking too big a backswing. Try moving inside the baseline and hitting balls as soon as they bounce. This will require a shorter backswing and a firm wrist on contact. Do everything else the same. Good. Much better. You are a bit loose on contact and placement.*

Charles — *It feels great. I'm sure I can do better in my next match. Let's play some.*

Nick — *Not yet. Let's work a little more. Practice and more practice develops habit. Move in more and let's see if you really have it. Stand on the service line area and practice the same shot.*

Charles — *What's so tough about that? If I did it from the baseline area, I can do it here.*

Nick — *Are you ready? Here it comes! What happened? You hit it into the net.*

Charles — *I wasn't ready. Bet you I get the next one.*

Nick — *You must get down to the level of the ball, bend the front knee and relax the back knee with your weight going forward.*

Charles — *It's much tougher here than I thought. The balls are at my feet with lots of pace. Not only do I have to cut down my backswing, but the ball has to go over the net. That's tough.*

Nick — *It's tough but not impossible. Do not try to hit this shot with too much power. Use the power from my ball.*

Charles — *That's fine, but they are so low.*

Nick — *I already explained to you that it is essential to get down to the level of the ball. Not only do you get down to the ball, but the racquet head must be up as much as possible with the face slightly open to lift the ball over the net.*

Charles — *I'm getting the idea, but so many of my balls go too high and are put away, especially in doubles.*

Nick — *It is important to clear the net and place the ball deep into your opponent's backcourt. At this time, do not get impatient with how high the balls are going. Control will improve by practice and learning to adjust the angle of the racquet head. Before we hit any more balls, let me emphasize the importance of getting down to the level of the ball. Some of the good players' front knees almost touch the ground when they make this shot. Too many novice players are too straight. They do not turn and instead end up scooping the ball. This places a great deal of strain on your wrist.*

Charles — *Just where do I meet the ball?*

Nick — *Try hitting the ball right after contact with the ground. The longer you wait, the more difficult it is to have timing and control.*

Charles — *What about my backhand side?*

Nick — *It's just about the same. Try using the left hand for added support whether you use a two-handed backhand or a one-handed. Remember, your wrist is extra firm to offset lack of strength.*

Charles — *This all sounds terrific until I actually play a match. Then everything changes. To think of these low balls is beyond me. I'm going to try to stay back on my baseline.*

Nick — *You can't stay there all the time. There are times you will have to hit this type of ball when you are caught out of position close to the baseline area. You have to practice this shot so you can use it during a match. It will come.*

Conclusion

When hitting a half-volley, imagine a target three to five feet from the baseline and inside the singles line. Aim for that spot and quickly move into the net after your shot. Hit down the line because you open up less of the court. Most returns will come back to your area so move in close. By moving in, you place pressure on your opponent to hit a good passing shot.

If your ball is hit entirely defensively, try scampering back to the baseline.

8

THE SERVE

The serve is considered by many to be the single most important stroke in tennis. It certainly sets the tempo at the start of every point and it can make or break you!

Throughout the years there have been players with booming serves: Arthur Ashe, Roscoe Tanner, John Newcombe, John Alexander and Virginia Wade. There have also been great players with less power, but well-placed and consistent serves such as the master, Ken Rosewall.

Many players can perfect one serve, but John Newcombe was able to master a variety of serves. In addition, he believed serving with all-out power was not necessary. He served just hard enough to allow him to win with consistency. Arthur Ashe, on the other hand, exerted full power on his first serve, resulting in more outright winners.

I do not recommend you copy either Ashe or Newcombe. But whichever, I strongly suggest you have an excellent second serve to back up the misses of your first ball. If I had to select just one stroke to determine how good a player was at a first glance, it would be a second serve in the tie breaker of the final set. The poise, confidence and ability of a player are tested more by this one shot than by any other. The second serve — with depth and accuracy — is a must for **all** players.

There are four basic serves: the flat, slice, spin and twist. Each is effective and each travels differently to your opponent. To be a complete server, I emphasize a good flat, slice, and spin serve, in the manner of Newcombe. However, if you were restricted to a consistent first and second well-placed spin or slice serve you could still be a champion.

To hit these different serves requires few changes in the serving motion, toss and grip. However, small adjustments are made to achieve more spin or velocity.

Flat Serve

The flat or cannonball serve uses either the Continental or Eastern Forehand grip. This grip allows the player to hit the ball fairly flat and with a great amount of speed.

The toss for this serve is a little to the right, out in front of the body, and to a height that will have the player reach to full extension. This toss is the best place for the cannonball serve since this is the area where the most power is achieved.

The flat serve is used primarily as a first serve. If hit and placed correctly, it can be a devastating weapon. Remember, this serve is not a high percentage serve so a spin serve is a must for a second serve.

Slice

The slice serve is probably one of the best serves to have in your repertoire. In fact, if a player could have only one serve, I would like him to use the slice serve. It is very dependable and can be placed with great accuracy and is very effective when hit correctly. The ball stays low and curves in flight making it difficult to return.

To hit the slice serve takes only a slight adjustment from hitting a flat serve. First, toss the ball a little more to the right of the flat serve, about two o'clock. Second, you'll have to brush the ball instead of hitting it flat. Hit the ball more on the right side and follow through around the ball. Third, to hit the slice serve an Eastern Backhand grip is very helpful. It will help produce the brushing motion with very little effort. Fourth, remember to hit up on the ball. Getting full extension is important even on slice and spin serves. Remember, slice serves tend to go down and to the left so aim deeper and hit a bit longer.

Spin Serve

The spin or topspin serve is another great addition to your game. Like the slice serve, the spin serve adds consistency and percentage to your game. It also gives variety and places doubt upon the receiver. But the greatest advantage of this serve is the high, deep bounce and high net clearance.

To hit the topspin serve, the player should again use the Eastern Backhand grip. Try tossing the ball a little to the left of the flat serve or about eleven o'clock. Then brush up and over the ball from left to right, following through around the left side. Extension is still important. If you are cramped, the ball will not bounce as high and you may not get the desired velocity. Reach up and hit spin serves with confidence.

Twist

This serve I leave for others to teach. I feel it leads to back problems and the disadvantages outweight its advantages. If you're interested in this serve, I suggest you consider the possible long-term physical risk before you pursue it.

No matter which serve you use, unless you are tall and fall into the category of Chip Hooper, my student who stands at 6-feet-6 plus a 110" racquet, you must hit up and out on the ball — not directly down.

The following series of lessons will discuss and illustrate my approach to a beginner and advancing the player through the intermediate and, finally, advanced level of play.

Please note I will not attempt to integrate shoulder turns, body flex, elbow height, etc., in a complicated manner, but will give simple suggestions to attain the same needed ingredients for a successful serve.

Before thinking my method is different and perhaps contrary to yours, keep in mind, I have learned to transfer one or two simple hints that might help you without making a major change. There are certain basics for all, but each person has limitations and capabilities worked within their framework.

The following are important key points to remember about the serve:

1. Grip. Beginners can start with an Eastern Forehand and as they develop strength and confidence, adjust this grip to a Continental-Eastern Backhand. Adjustments will be uncomfortable but are necessary to acquire a consistent serve with spin.

2. Ready Position. There are several opinions to this position. Apply the one that seems most comfortable to you.

    A. Weight forward, shift backward and then forward.

    B. Evenly balanced and forward.

    C. Weight back and shift forward.

3. Toss. I suggest you hold one ball lightly in your finger tips. Hold on to the ball until the arm is fully extended and then release. **NOTE:** Fewer body movements will help control the toss.

Varied swing patterns for the Spin, Flat, Slice serves.

4. Backswing. The ball and racquet should work together in the downswing, upswing and on contact. The downswing should be a continuous motion with no hitches. Be sure to work on a full backswing. (If you are unable to learn this, there are many successful servers on all levels who abbreviate the backswing, especially those having difficulty controlling the toss and racquet arm.)

   A few good checkpoints are to have your racquet fairly close to your body on the downswing, and then reach for the fence; bend the arm with the racquet head going up and then down to the famous back-scratching position. (**NOTE:** I do not insist that you get that racquet all the way down. Level of play will tell who can do it.)

5. Contact with ball. The perfect spot is to contact the ball at a point where the arm and racquet are fully extended. Too high a toss causes a hitch waiting for the ball. Too low a toss makes it difficult to hit up and out and also to have full extension.

6. Follow through. The same applies to the serve as that of groundstrokes.

   A. Too short a follow-through means you slowed down before contact with the ball.

   B. Follow through to your left-hand side. With this follow-through, you have made contact with confidence.

The Basic Service Lesson

Nick — *Pearson and Louis, I plan to work with both of you to-day on your serve.*

Pearson and Louis — *Gee, we thought forehand and backhands had to be mastered before going to the serve.*

Nick — *Groundstrokes are very important, but the serve should be part of your first lessons. There is no reason to think any basic stroke (forehand, backhand, serve, volley) should linger behind. True, you may be a bit young at 8 and 9 to develop a cannonball like Ashe, but we will learn the basics of a serve. As you get older, additions will be made.*

Let's stand by the service line area to start with. As you begin to get the idea we will move back to the baseline.

(NOTE: Standing a little closer to the net makes it easier for the student to hit the ball over the net. Even though you work on the same steps from the service line, youngsters and some adults use excessive motions and muscle instead of a relaxed swing. At times, I have some of my most advanced students move to this area for a basic refresher.)

Put your racquets down and throw the ball to me a few times.

Pearson and Louis — *That's baseball!*

Nick — *Right on. I want you to imitate the same motion of your favorite pitcher or infielder throwing the ball. Louis, that's perfect. Pearson, look at Louis a few times and observe how he turns his shoulder when taking the ball back. Look how relaxed he is with his arm and especially the snap of the wrist when releasing the ball. Too many people push the ball when throwing or hitting a serve. Better, much better. Now move back to the baseline and throw me the ball. Louis, that's great. Pearson, you threw down. Try throwing the ball up and out. It will come down so don't worry. Come back to the service line and let's continue with our next step. Place your arm and racquet above your shoulder. Good, lower the racquet head just a little. Simply throw the ball up slightly and try hitting it over the net with your Eastern Forehand grip. Don't worry where it goes.*

(NOTE: I have said nothing about the importance of the toss or backswing at this point even though these are fundamental elements. All I am trying to do is develop confidence in hitting the ball with a relaxed motion. Where it goes, I don't care. Too much advice at this point is beyond their comprehension. I recommend the Eastern Forehand grip because youngsters, and some adults, lack strength. Most feel more secure with this grip. Of course, as quickly as possible, I suggest a switch to the Continental or Eastern Backhand. These grips place the racquet head in a difficult position and require stronger wrists.)

Pearson and Louis — *Did you see that? I hit my balls over. All of them. Are you mad because they are going past the baseline?*

Nick — *I will never get mad whenever you hit groundstrokes or serves long. Okay. Put your racquets on the ground and let's toss the ball for awhile. Remember the following: Hold the ball lightly in your fingers. Hold one ball at a time. This will give you the opposite hand to hold your racquet if your serve goes in. It's very important for those with two-handed backhand to cut down on those body motions when tossing.*

Pearson
and Louis — *How high do we toss it?*

Nick — *Don't worry about that. But if you can throw the ball as high as your arm and racquet extended, it would be great.*
(NOTE: Again, do not worry at this point. I just hinted at the height. That will do the trick most of the time.)

Pearson
and Louis — *Can we serve some balls?*

Nick — *You sure can. Let's play follow the leader. Let's stand on the service line. You are going to hit six balls the same as I do.*
First two balls — *My racquet is above my right shoulder with the racquet head down slightly and elbow fairly high. The ball is down and fairly close to the inside of my left leg.*
Second two balls — *My racquet and ball start out in front of my body, waist high. The ball and racquet come down very slowly until they reach the same position as when hitting the first two balls, then they stop.*
Last two balls — *Start out the same as position two, but continue down, up and hit in one motion.*

Pearson
and Louis — *Wow, that was so tough, especially the last two balls. I couldn't even hit the ball.*

Nick — *Why not?*

Pearson — *The ball was too far behind me.*

Louis — *One ball was too far in front and my other ball was too far to the left.*

Nick — *You both did fairly well for the first time, but can you both tell me what you feel is really important in developing a good serve?*

Pearson
and Louis — *The toss!*

73

Nick — *Right, one hundred percent right. Put your racquets down on the ground like mine is. The racquet head is slightly to the left of the right foot and about 1 to 1 1/2 feet in front of your body. Let's see how many tosses it takes before we can hit the face of the racquet. Try to remember what we talked about. Let your tossing hand be straight up before releasing the ball. Hold your balls lightly in your fingers. Don't jump around when tossing the ball. Stand fairly straight, relax, but do not bend your knees or arch your body.*

Pearson — *But I see the pros arch when they serve.*

Nick — *That will come in time. Come on, let's do it together. Great, keep it up. Good, you have it!*

Pearson
and Louis — *I got it. I thought everyone said the serve was so tough.*

Nick — *Parts of the game may be difficult but if you learn stroke production and you practice until a habit is formed, you can do it all. Now that we are getting this idea, you can move back a step or two. If you maintain the rhythm and timing you now have, you will soon be serving from the baseline. Don't forget, serve up and out!*

The Intermediate Service Lesson

Nick — *Pearson and Louis, I have enjoyed working with both of you the past few years and feel a great deal of progress has been accomplished in all areas.*

Pearson
and Louis — *We are happy too, except if we don't get our first serve in, our opponents often put away our second serve.*

Nick — *Can you tell me why? Remember to explain very simply what you do.*

Pearson
and Louis — *We try to hit the first serve hard and if we miss, we make sure the second goes in by hitting it much easier. A few years ago we did well; but now that we're playing tournaments we seem to be off balance when they return the second serve.*

Nick — *Please listen to me very closely. It is important to develop a solid first and second serve. The first does not have to be a cannonball — nor does the second have to be a powder puff. Let's try to make our first and second serve just about the same. When you get to be*

16-18 years old, your physical development will determine your serve. Serve a few balls for me, hitting the first and second with the same power. Okay, stop! It is important to understand that you are old enough to make slight adjustments with your grips. You are both using the Eastern Forehand grip, a little more to your left. Try a few. Do everything the same.

Pearson — *I feel too weak with this grip.*

Louis — *I seem to lose power.*

Nick — *You both are absolutely right, but the power will be offset by slice (spin).*

Pearson
and Louis — *Will we get that power back some day?*

Nick — *Yes, power will develop in time, but try to remember power is not the key to success.*

Pearson
and Louis — *With this grip, I seem to hit around the ball too much and it's not even going near the serve box.*

Nick — *With this grip, make believe you are hitting a flat serve.* (NOTE: By making them hit the same as with the Eastern Forehand, they will attempt to hit a flat serve but because of their new grip they will go up and brush the ball, applying spin for the first time. There will be difficulty in the beginning with the new grip but practice will overcome that feeling.)

Pearson
and Louis — *We seem to be hitting many of our balls into the net.*

Nick — *You must hit up and out. Let's play a game. Watch me. I am going to kneel on the ground with my right knee touching. In order to get the ball over the net, I must hit up and out.*

Pearson
and Louis — *We'll try, but that looks tough.*

Nick — *With your new grip, think of throwing your racquet up at the ball. Don't think of anything but up and out.*

Pearson
and Louis — *We can't do it. It's too difficult to get power with this position and our racquets keep hitting the ground.*

Nick — *Let the racquet head accelerate, relax your wrist on contact. You can't force a serve. Relax! Relax! Hit up and out!*

Pearson
and Louis — *Look, it went over! Another, another!*

Nick — *Stand up and do exactly the same over and over. Great! Great! Notice the height and depth of the ball along with spin for the first time. By the way, the spin will bring the ball down into the box. Before leaving, review these check points. Use a grip as close to an Eastern backhand as possible. It will take time to be comfortable with this grip, but hitting dozens of serves each day will overcome that. Hit up and out and do not force this serve. Relax and let your racquet do the work.*

The Advanced Service Lesson

Nick — *Louis, after two years, it's sort of strange not having you and Pearson together, but now that you are a tournament player, all efforts must be made to strengthen your serve.*

Louis — *Even though I'm almost 15, some of the other boys have much more power. My first serve is better, but the second is still shaky. I know one reason is my Dad does not let me use station training to build up the upper part of my body.*

Nick — *I am not going to say right or wrong to your Dad's decision. But there are other methods to build strength and I feel your serve can improve by the following:*

  1. Proper toss — Before releasing your ball, you have a tendency to cup your fingers, causing the ball to go to your left side too much.
  2. When hitting the ball that far left, it is very difficult to get the benefit of body weight.

Louis — *I feel like my ball is in front.*

Nick — *On your next few tosses, let the ball drop.*

Louis — *Gosh, I don't believe it. The ball is about two feet to the left of my left foot. Can you help me correct that?*

Nick — *Perhaps the single most important factor of the serve is the toss.*

Basic Fundamentals

• *Do not let go of the ball until your arm is fully extended.*

• *Do not hold your ball tightly. Hold it lightly by your fingers; primarily the thumb, index and middle fingers.*

Remembering and practicing the above will help place the toss of the ball in the same spot most of the time (slightly to the right of your left foot and about 1½ feet in front

Advanced Serve Motion: Note extension of left arm.

of you.) (NOTE: This toss will also get you to the net a step or two quicker.)

Louis, I want you to throw a few balls for me. Notice how you bend your knees and turn your shoulder before releasing the ball?

Louis — *What's that mean?*

Nick — *Very seldom do I ever mention much about body movements, but the serve movement does require explanation. When you serve the ball, you stand very straight throughout the entire serve motion and have no shoulder rotation at all. When you threw the balls for me, you did the opposite. Your right shoulder actually pivoted and you pushed with your legs for power. Do the very same with your racquet this time. Don't worry where the ball goes. Think of actually throwing your racquet up and out to the ball.*

Louis — *That feels a little better.*

Nick — *Not good enough for me. I want you to do the following: don't think I'm crazy, but throw your racquet in the same motion that you threw the ball. (NOTE: Don't try this unless you are on a soft court.) Great! Do it again, again. Now, hit the ball the very same way. THAT'S IT! You did it!*

Louis — *I can't believe it. More power and action without even trying.*

Nick — *Just one more little tip and you're ready. Accelerate your forearm and wrist. Louis, on the upper part of your serve, you should think of one thing; go up after that ball and let the racquet head hit it. To do this you must step up the forward thrust of your forearm and wrist before and throughout contact. Too many players slow down and only guide the racquet to the ball.*

Louis — *Give me a hint to improve this.*

Nick — *Very simple. Throw me the ball without any speed-up action of your forearm and wrist. Now, repeat that same throw, but increase the speed just before releasing the ball. Good! Pick up your racquet and do the very same motions.*

Louis — *I don't believe the difference. It's so easy.*

Nick — *So many players on all levels of play forget that muscle is not the key to success. Serving is easy if you remember the basic tips.*

Conclusion

Serving is certainly a very basic element of the game and any successful player must be confident and secure with both first and second serves. While each individual will develop personal habits that may prove effective, the following general review points should help everyone. Study these points and put them into practice and your service game should improve.

1. The serve is considered the key to modern tennis.
2. The serve should be offensive and start the control of that point.
3. Lack of power can be offset by movement of your ball to different positions as best illustrated by Ken Rosewall.
4. There are four types of serve: Flat, slice, spin and twist.
5. Ready position:
    A. Weight forward
    B. Weight evenly balanced
    C. Weight on rear foot
6. In the ready position, it is essential to be relaxed.
7. The ball and racquet must work together developing a smooth rhythm.
8. Minimum body motion, especially in the low to medium level, helps control the toss and timing.
9. Bending of the knees helps add power.
10. The flat cannonball serve gives power, but second serve usually determines the match. Slice serve offers control, bounces low

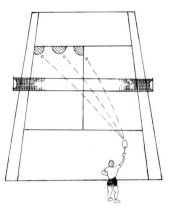

Serve Placement is as important as power. Deep serves that make your opponents move or jam him can be as effective as an extra 20 MPH of velocity.

and away from a right-handed opponent's forehand forcing them off the court.

11. Weight transfer is largely determined by the angle of the front foot. John McEnroe defies this production, but gets away with it by turning his entire body.

12. The toss often determines the success of the serve.

13. For lower levels of tennis, I suggest you hold only one ball because:
    A. Free hand is small and is often used for two-handed backhands.
    B. Players have a tendency to rush the first serve when holding both balls.

14. Hold ball lightly in fingers.

15. Extend arm completely before releasing the ball — it adds control.

16. Start with ball and racquet approximately waist-high to develop rhythm. If started too low, racquet hand must rush to catch up with ball.

17. Too low a toss — difficult for reaching action. Too high — racquet must wait for ball which breaks up rhythm.

18. Body flex, body arc help develop power and a kick on the ball. A small percentage of players have flex. Most players stand fairly straight, making it difficult to have a powerful flat, slice, kick serve.

19. Hitting UP and OUT are essential!
20. Shoulder rotation applied by baseball pitchers and quarterbacks is essential to the serve; without this rotation, you are hitting the serve with arm only.
21. Muscle force is not necessary. The relaxed body, arm and a wrist snap is the key to a successful serve.
22. The serve should not have hitches but should be one fluent motion.
23. Trying to force a serve will result in upper body injuries.

9

OVERHEAD

The overhead can be one of the most exhilarating strokes in tennis. As the ball floats down into the range of a player waiting to pounce on it, you can often feel the excitement building.

But that exhilaration can quickly turn to agony if the soft floating plum is not picked correctly. Too often what should be a clear winner turns to disaster. The majority of overheads are missed because of two reasons: lack of confidence and poor execution.

When you're practicing overheads, put the shot into perspective by remembering that if you can hit a serve, you can hit an overhead. True you have only one chance to hit the shot and you have to move underneath the lob. The key elements of the stroke are so similar that you should quickly master the shot and hit it for winners.

The following are important overhead practice tips:

1. The overhead requires moving your feet, making good position and executing the shot.

2. This shot is an offensive weapon and is often a straight out winner. Move in quickly for a possible defensive return.

3. Trying to muscle the ball or use too much body will result in mis-hits.

4. This stroke often divides players into two distinct categories:

   A. Average player fears the overhead and often plays the ball on a bounce.

Left hand and racquet prepare together.

Racquet goes behind head.

Head and eyes are up and arm is fully extended on contact.

Follow-through completes the confident overhead.

       B. The tournament player takes full advantage of this shot and hits offensive shots and winners.

5.   The serve and overhead are very similar except:

      A. **Serve**
         1. two chances
         2. standing still
         3. you control the toss
         4. a full backswing

      B. **Overhead**
         1. one chance
         2. requires movement for position
         3. not enough time for full backswing

6.   The left hand and racquet should go up at the same time you start moving for the ball.

7.   Utilize the left hand to point at ball which lifts both sides of the body. Be sure to keep the left hand up as long as possible. This will help prevent opening up the hitting stance too soon, or pulling down your left side which could result in a mis-hit.

8.   Reach up for the ball. Do not let it drop.

9.   Use very little effort and motion from the upper part of the body.

10.   Head should be up, looking at the ball, even after contact.

11.   There is no such shot as a defensive overhead.

12.   Do not concern yourself with placement in the beginning. Hit balls to the big portion of the court.

13.   There are two methods of going back or forward for the ball:

      A. Side step — good for a few steps.

      B. Leg crossover — covers distance quicker.

14.   Be ready to move fast and make position. If in doubt, move back an additional step and then come forward.

15.   Try not to leave your feet in the beginning of the overhead, though there are times you must leave the ground to make contact with the ball.

16.   Turn sideways. Get your racquet and left hand up immediately.

17.   Continental to Eastern Backhand are the preferred grips.

18.   Recover quickly after overheads to capitalize on weak returns.

The Lesson

Nick — *Stephen, your game has improved a great deal the past six months. Do you feel any part of your game needs* a little extra attention?

Stephen — *I do not look forward to hitting an overhead.*

Nick — *Why do you feel this is a trouble area?*

Stephen — *There is so much involved in an overhead. I find it difficult to judge the position of the ball. When I finally reach it, everything goes wrong.*

Nick — *There is no reason to fear any shot. But you must be open and positive before attempting any stroke.*

Stephen — *That's easy for you to say. I let my balls bounce and then hit an overhead.*

Nick — *By doing this, you often let your opponent off the hook. Let's try hitting overheads on all my lobs. Don't let them bounce. Hey, that's not bad at all. Here comes another. Hold it, hold it!*

Stephen — *For the first time I hit a few overheads and you say "Hold it!"*

Nick — *You may hit a few more overheads, but there are basics that should be followed in order to become consistent. First, turn sideways the moment you think overhead. Second, while turning, lift the left hand and racquet hand into position.*

These two simple points will give you an excellent chance of hitting the overhead.

Stephen — *Why do I lift the left hand? It doesn't hit the ball.*

Nick — *The left hand is important. It tracks the ball and the left side of the body must also reach up.*

Stephen — *Is my grip OK?*

Nick — *Yes, you hit the overhead with the Continental grip. I suggest this grip because it requires no change from the volley. The backhand grip is also used. Arthur Ashe prefers this because his spin adds control to the shot. I do not disagree, but feel a great many players have a tendency to hit their overheads crosscourt with this grip. Also there is a loss of strength, especially in medium-level players.*

Stephen — *I'm beginning to feel a little more confident, but I still mis-hit a lot of my balls on the top of the frame.*

Nick — *You and other players do the same movements. Watch me very closely as I hit the next few overheads.*

Stephen — *When you stand up and reach for the ball and stay that way throughout the overhead, you seem to hit it perfectly.*

Nick — *You're right. Try to remember these suggestions:*
1. *Reach up with entire body, including the racquet and left hand.*
2. *Do not try to force power with the upper part of your body.*
3. *Let the racquet and arm do all the work.*
4. *If you pull down when making contact, the racquet will also come down. This will cause a mishit. Many players, especially females, are frightened to extend; the very same thing pertains to the serve.*

Stephen — *You're right. I watched a television match with a young player from India.*

Nick — *You mean Ramish Krishnon.*

Stephen — *That's him. After hitting an overhead his head and left hand still were extended upward.*

Nick — *An overhead is a beautiful and graceful stroke when executed correctly. It is even more exciting when a player is forced to jump because of an excellent offensive lob. The entire body extends upward getting that extra few inches from the legs in a scissors kick motion.*

Stephen — *At times, I also find it difficult to judge the ball.*

Nick — *When in doubt move an extra step backward. It is always easier to make a last-second adjustment coming forward.*

Stephen — *What about my backswing? Is it the same as the serve?*

Nick — *I suggest a shorter backswing on the overhead because you are moving to the ball. Lift the racquet directly upward to the shoulder area.*

Stephen — *What about my footwork?*

Nick — *I say very little about this until difficulty arises. However, I suggest you side-step for the overhead that is fairly close to you and leg crossover for the others. Use the same as an outfielder running down a line drive.*

Stephen — *What happens if my overhead is not too offensive?*

Nick — *React very quickly:*
1. *Move into the net. This will alarm your opponent and, hopefully, force an error.*
2. *Many people, even after hitting an offensive overhead, stay in the same location. By doing this, you place no pressure on your opponent. You must move. Overhead and attack.*

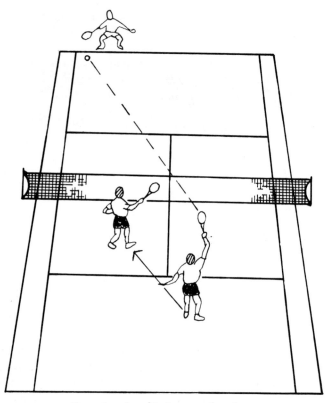

Move in after hitting overhead.

Conclusion

While a good player seems to crack overheads with perfect ease, remember, nothing in tennis comes without practice. The winners smashed during a match represent hours of mis-hits during practice.

Thousands of balls have to be hit in practice to achieve the consistency needed during match play. Too often, players shy away from the overhead because they try it once or twice with disastrous results and never try another. But like any other shot, practice makes perfect.

While you're getting the basics of this shot, don't make the mistake of trying for too much power. Power is not the only factor to a successful overhead. Placement is extremely important and you must have full extension at contact and follow through with confidence.

Finally, remember — there is no such thing as half-an-overhead. When you make up your mind on the overhead, hit it.

10

RETURN OF SERVICE

In order to win a match you must break service at some point. To do that requires a good service return. The return of serve is often thought of as the **second most important stroke in tennis.** Yet in spite of the importance of this shot, it is practiced the least of any stroke.

Throughout most practice sessions, players will trade groundstroke for groundstroke, volley for volley, hit lobs and overheads and practice their serves. But the only time they hit return of serves is when they play practice sets or matches. And even then they don't practice the return as much as they hit the ball to keep it in play.

Unless you are an exception, you cannot become confident with a shot unless you hit the same stroke thousands of times. But because of this lack of practice, you will find it difficult to break your opponent's serve.

You should remember this point: The return of serve will gain or lose control of that point.

If you improve your return of service, it automatically gives you a psychological boost; the weapon of the opponent has been nullified. In effect you are taking the punch out of your opponent's serve and immediately going on the offensive. This forces the opponent to go at you with baseline rallies, a strategy which alone will cause unforced errors.

While I personally feel strongly about a strong service return, there is another school of thought which stresses getting the ball back in play as the single most important factor, especially early in the match. The thought is that by getting the ball back, you will have time to pick up momentum, confidence and do more with the return midway in the match.

I suggest you follow a plan with which you feel confident. But whatever your selection it requires practice. The following are some suggestions plus practice drills to help your return of serve.

The Grip

The choice of grip is often determined by your receiving position. The majority of players I have worked with use the forehand grip, especially against hard servers.

If you are confused, maintain the grip you feel gives you the most strength.

Position To Return Service

No one cay say what is right or wrong position to return service. Quite often players go with their most consistent, powerful stroke which causes them to favor a particular side.

John Newcombe, when returning from the advantage side, would stand in the alley letting you know he was going to crunch your serve. His confidence caused a great many double faults. However, despite personal preference, I suggest that advanced players stay close to the singles line while intermediate players divide the baseline in half; perhaps favoring their best stroke a little more.

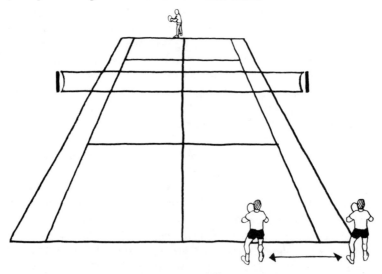

Adjust your position to force the serve to hit to your strength.

(NOTE: If you start working on return of serve in the early stage of play, you will do extremely well in all levels of your advancement. Advanced players feel more comfortable leaving the middle open because after returning service when served to the middle they are at the center of the baseline.)

Ready Position

The serve — for the most part — will have speed on the first ball and spin on the second ball. Because of this, I suggest:

A. First Serve — Have your racquet quite low in the ready position to handle the low fast bounce.

B. Second Serve — Racquet waist high to prepare for a higher bounce.

Not only is it important to have your racquet ready, but your body should also be prepared to spring in any direction. It is not necessary to crouch with your knees almost touching the ground to hit a good return. In fact you may be upright. The main factor is weight forward. Make sure your knees are relaxed, weight is forward, and your eyes are glued on the opponent's racquet when it makes contact with the ball.

A good ready position could possibly tell you what type of serve is coming at you because you will be concentrating on your opponent. Watch the ball toss; if it varies, so will the serve.

Playing Surface

A. Clay or Slow Surface — Your opponent will be hesitant to attack. Your returns should be deep, applying pressure at all times. Whether you go crosscourt or down the lines should be determined before the ball arrives.

B. Faster Surface (grass, concrete) — The serve and volley game will force you to return balls much lower.

Meeting Ball in Front
(Shorter Backswing, Proper Body Balance)

At times, balls will come at you in excess of 100 miles-per-hour; 60 miles-per-hour in the intermediate level.

Quick reactions are needed. Make sure your weight is forward and you make contact in front. Cut down your backswing like Vitas Gerulaitis, Jimmy Connors and Gene Mayer.

The short backswing is offset by your weight going forward and a big follow-through. Be sure to hold your racquet firmly in event of mis-hits. Many players will stop on a mis-hit, but follow through all the time. Right or wrong, get into the habit of finishing all your strokes.

Variations on Return of Service

Except for the top players, I recommend very simple forehand and backhand groundstrokes for service returns. The only difference is a smaller backswing.

With daily practice and getting to know your opponent's serve, you can vary the return with:

A. Drop shots
B. Running around the second serve and hitting a big forehand or backhand, depending on which is your stronger stroke.
C. Attacking the serve when least expected. (When you attack be sure to keep the ball in play.)

Vary Your Position When Returning Serve

At times, especially if Roscoe Tanner is having a big day with his first serve, try breaking his concentration by standing in different positions. It may not help, but it probably won't hurt. When your opponent's serve is hot, you have nothing to lose.

Best Return Against Flat and Spin Serves

A. Flat — Do nothing more than block the ball. A single block, holding the racquet firmly, will get the ball back.
B. Spin — You must hit through a spin serve. Just blocking it will steer the ball out of bounds. When you're having trouble with a spin serve, wait for the ball and hit the return to the big portion of the court or even crosscourt.

(NOTE: Concentrate on only one thing; the ball! The ball! Do not watch what the server is doing. Watch the ball and get it back even if you have to kick it.)

Outright Winners — Solid Consistent Returns
Varieties of Service

A. Jimmy Connors:

A few years ago, Brian Gottfried, a student of mine for many years, was playing Jimmy at Flushing Meadows. Jimmy was up two sets to one, but Brian was leading the fourth set and was up 40-15. Brian served and volleyed four times in a row. But each time the return of serve was better and better. Connors finally hit three outright winners and put a fourth at Brian's feet. That ended the match!

Jimmy has the ability to hit the ball on the run with excellent timing. He concentrates every second and is determined to drive the ball back every time. He does not have to hit outright winners all the time but he applies pressure with every return.

B.   Rod Laver:

Rod could hurt you each and every time with a different return. His ability to control his wrist and racquet were outstanding. The opponent never knew what to expect.

C.   Gene Mayer:

With two hands from both sides, he is able to bring the ball down which causes opponents to hit up on their volley.

D.   Jimmy Arias/John Newcombe:

Daring you to come close to their forehand returns which are often hit for outright winners.

E.   Ken Rosewall:

Considered by many as the King of Service Return. His returns were not winners and some were even a little defensive but he applied constant pressure with pin-pointed returns. The pressure generated by his returns was the turning point of many of his matches.

(NOTE: My recommendation: Copy Ken Rosewall's return, because with an excellent return you can finish the point on your opponent's defensive shot.)

Women's Tennis

For the most part, especially on second serve, women do not serve and volley but elect to stay in the baseline area. With this in mind, remember the following:

A.   Make sure your return moves the server. Test her forehand and backhand, seeking a weak point, and exploit that weakness on return of service. Do not go for outright winners. Concentrate on solid placements, an occasional short return, then go for the big portion of the court for the point.

B.   On second serves go for placements and short returns, or drop shots. Many women do not want to come in and, when forced, you can pass or lob for the point.

C.   Attack their serves. Usually hit down the line and alternate deep down the center shots. This causes confusion about what side to play the ball.

D.   Show the server you are confident in handling her serve. Look confident. Be aggressive when you make your returns.

11

LOB

More than any other shot the lob is misunderstood, misused or just plain missed. Many players, even top touring professionals, resist the lob because they feel it is not aggressive tennis, totally ignoring the lob's offensive characteristics. Then there are times the lob is used incorrectly, often causing a lost point more from shot selection than execution. And, of course, who hasn't lofted a ball far beyond the baseline? No shot looks worse than a lob that backfires.

Yet, I feel the lob, along with the drop shot, is one of the most underrated strokes in tennis. This statement pertains to all levels of play.

The lob should be a part of your game precisely because it is so basic. The lob is nothing but a groundstroke hit with the racquet face slightly open on contact. You do not have to change the backswing, grip or for the most part, the forward part of the stroke.

Used defensively, the lob should be the shot of choice when you're off balance or pushed off the court. It is quite disheartening for most players to see one of their offensively hit shots returned with a high deep lob. Such a shot may cause the attacker to be impatient and go for a bigger shot too soon.

The offensive lob, which is identical to a forehand-backhand groundstroke except for added height, can be used with great success if your opponent puts pressure on you at the net. Those players who stick their noses over the net will have to do a lot of about-faces if the offensive or topspin lob is part of your shot repertoire.

The lob, used in conjunction with your other shots, adds variety and versatility to your game. It's an essential element that can win you a point or just plain buy you some time. Either way, the lob should be an instrumental part of everyone's game.

The Defensive Lob

The defensive lob is the most widely recognized and used shot in the lob family. It looks similar to any other lob and the stroking pattern is the same as the other groundstrokes with the face more open on contact. In teaching the defensive lob, little is mentioned about any change in the stroke.

The defensive lob, which is the shot most disdained by some players as non-aggressive, should be used when your opponent has hit an offensive shot that moves you out of position or when you try an offensive shot that turns out not to be too offensive. When your opponent is attacking and rushing the net, a well-placed lob will give you the opportunity to regain your position or balance.

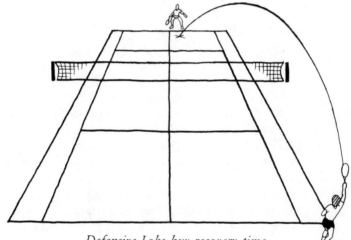

Defensive Lobs buy recovery time.

There are four elements of the defensive lob to remember:
1. Get your racquet head back in position.
2. Hit through that forehand and backhand with a little less power.
3. Get under the ball and hit from a low to a high point.
4. Keep your wrist firm on contact.

Forehand Lob

The Lesson

Nick — *Kellie, let's rally from the baseline hitting both forehands and backhands, remembering to hit from a low to a high point and maintain a firm wrist on contact.*

Try to get the balls to go a little higher over the net and keep the ball on the racquet longer. Now, Kellie, let's play a game with our forehands and backhands. See if you can hit the ball as high as my racquet and arm extended up at the net position and how deep you can place it into the backcourt.

Keep hitting the ball high above the net, using your forehand and backhand in your normal groundstroking fashion. Open the face slightly on contact with a little higher follow-through. That's it, Kellie, you're hitting your lobs extremely well today. Keep in mind to hit those shots just about the same except with less power.

Kellie — *What do you mean? I was hitting my groundstrokes.*

Nick — *That's right, Kellie. A lob is nothing more than a groundie hit with the face slightly open on contact. When the ball is hit higher than your opponent's outstretched arm and racquet, you're hitting a lob.*

The Offensive Lob

Many people feel the lob is one-dimensional, namely, defensive, and forget or ignore the other side of the shot. I like to remind them that a mortar fires rounds in a high lob trajectory and it is an offensive weapon.

Like a mortar shell, a well-placed and delivered lob is as effective a shot as there is in tennis. Anyone who has faced the helpless feeling of having to turn and run down a perfect lob can attest to the scoring potential of the shot.

Like any lob, the offensive lob is almost identical to a forehand-backhand groundstroke except for added height when clearing the net.

You use the offensive lob when your opponent constantly moves in close to the net and you can put the ball over his head, hitting the ball just over his outstretched arm, especially with control and accuracy. It's a shot you should always be ready to use.

Hit the Offensive Lob just over the outstretched arm of your opponent.

When hitting the offensive lob, remember:
1. Maintain the same backswing as used in your regular groundstroke.
2. Wrist firm on contact.
3. Hit the stroke with the racquet face slightly open on contact.
4. Follow through.

The Lesson

Nick — *Kellie, today I want to hit forehand and backhand crosscourts and I want the balls to land deep into my backcourt. I know we've been working on these shots for some time — you're very good at them. But I want you to do exactly what you've been doing. The only difference is I want a little variation. Hit some of your groundies a little higher over the net. That's fine, Kellie. Now let's have a little fun. Whenever you hit a short groundie, I'll run up to the net and try winning the point with a volley. I want you to see if you can win with a passing shot.*

Kellie — *And if I don't win with a passing shot?*

Nick — *Try getting it over my head. Stroking the ball over my head, especially when you are controlling the ball, makes it impossible for me to reach it. You don't hit the ball any differently. You only have to hit it higher. You can hit an offensive lob as easily as any other groundstroke.*

Use the Offensive Lob to stop net rushers.

Many players feel the quickest line between two points is a straight line — the passing shot. But remember, the offensive lob is another weapon in your arsenal. Without it, you're limiting yourself needlessly. The shot is nearly identical to your other groundstrokes. Use it. By the way, it will make your passing shots more effective as the opponent will be in doubt as to whether you are going to pass or lob.

The Topspin Lob

The topspin lob is an advanced stroke but one that deserves discussion because it is very effective. Most players and students feel the secret of the topspin lob is the rollover wrist on contact. However, that is wrong. If it were the rollover wrist that made the shot, 99 percent of the world's tennis players could never master the technique.

The secret to hitting the topspin lob is actually a quick, sharp brushing movement when the racquet makes contact with the ball. The wrist may roll over after contact is made, but only after the shot has already been completed. Brushing the strings up the back of the ball with a crisp motion will put the spin on the ball. With the proper topspin, you'll find it possible not only to get the ball over your opponent, but to have it stay in bounds as well.

When hitting a topspin lob, remember:
1. Your backswing is the same as that for a forehand.
2. The racquet head gets far below the ball.
3. Keep wrist firm on contact.
4. Brush the back of the ball upward with a little acceleration.
5. Follow through to complete the stroke. Don't worry if the wrist rolls over after contact.

The Lesson

Nick — *Kellie, today let's have some fun and work on a different shot. Let's start by hitting 20 crosscourt forehands, clearing the net by three to five feet. That's fine, Kellie, now let's bring them a little higher, five to ten feet over the net. Good. Now, for the work. Get your racquet head far under the ball, which will be the beginning of the topspin. And keep your wrist real firm on contact. Also, I want you to hit the ball harder.*

Kellie — *If I do that and it's high over the net, the balls will fly out.*

Nick — *Look at my next stroke and notice the face of my racquet. You see I keep it parallel to the ground. On contact I bring*

Forehand

Topspin Lob

Backhand

it up with a brushing motion on the back of the ball. And my wrist is firm on contact. This motion will put a topspin on the ball, lifting it over my head and landing deep in my backcourt. When you hit this shot, you may feel that your wrist is rolling over. But actually your wrist does not roll over until the ball leaves the racquet. Now you're hitting the ball harder, it's clearing my head and still coming in bounds. You're hitting the topspin lob.

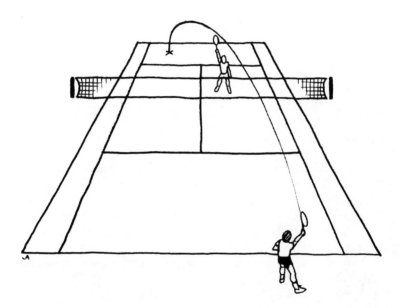

The Topspin Lob goes up and over opponent; chasing it down is almost impossible.

12

DROP SHOT

In my opinion, the drop shot and the lob are the two most underrated and least used strokes. Many players feel they are unfair. That is a foolish point of view. My feeling is that if these shots help win a match, they are more than fair to use. They are essential.

The drop shot is a short ball hit to your opponent. When hit well it should be a winner or force your opponent to move forward and return a defensive ball back to you.

The drop shot, once mastered, is very effective against most baseline players. Still, the intelligent player only uses the shot when in control of the ball. The drop shot is most effective when you are inside the court and your opponent is behind the baseline. Remember, your drop shot does not have to be an outright winner. Good placement may make the shot just as effective. Keeping your opponent off balance and moving in three directions instead of two could be a key to victory. Few players have used this shot more effectively than one past champion, Doris Hart, or current champion Chris Evert Lloyd.

Key Points to the Drop Shot
1. Preparation is the very same for a forehand or a backhand.
2. Do not hit from a low to a high. Hit from a high point to a low point and have the face of the racquet slightly open on contact.

3. Just before contact slow down; maintain a firm wrist at all times.
4. A slight lay-back of the wrist should be tried only after mastering the basic techniques of the stroke.
5. The follow-through is not as big as a regular groundstroke, but the racquet head should not stop on contact. Let it continue in the direction of the ball with the racquet face open.
6. Drop shots should normally be hit from several feet inside the baseline. But they can and should be tried from the baseline area on medium pace balls, especially when your opponent is out of position.

The Forehand Drop Shot

The face of the racquet is more open then on any of the groundstrokes.

The Backhand Drop Shot, notice the follow-through after contact.

The Lesson

Nick — *Let's have a playing lesson today.*

Raffaella — *Sounds great to me.*

Nick — *I really want you to think today. Instead of banging every ball, try to utilize the proper stroke at the right time. You serve! 0-15.*

Raffaella — *I thought we were going to play. You drop shotted me right off the bat.*

Nick — *Why not? You missed your first serve. And like most players, you're a little tight in the beginning of a match and you pushed your second serve in very short. You did not expect the drop shot which made it ideal for me to use. Serve again. 0-30.*

Raffaella — *My second serve was better, but I still lost.*

Nick — *It was better, but I placed my return deep and wide to your two-handed backhand. When you hit the short return, I hit a drop shot to the open side of the court and caught you off balance again. Your serve. Good. 15-30. You got your first serve in and controlled the ball throughout the entire point. 15-40. Once again. you got your first serve in but during the rally you hit an easy forehand inside the baseline, enabling me to drop shot. Drop shots will keep your opponent off guard. Serve again. My game. Because of my drop shots, you played the last point standing close to the baseline. Once I saw that, I hit my groundstrokes high and deep, causing your unforced error.*

Raffaella — *I never thought of the drop shot as being an offensive weapon.*

Nick — *It is not always an offensive weapon, but it can be utilized in many ways to get an offensive result. That versatility makes the drop shot so valuable. Let's talk awhile. Last week you lost a match that went three sets. But you did not take into account that your opponent was overweight and does not like to run up and back. But she hits extremely well when in position and you fell right into her game. You tried to slug with no variety at all. Even when she began to slow down in the second set and hit shallow balls you still went for outright winners. During the match the drop shot would have accomplished several things. Your opponent would have become very tired trying to cover the short balls. It is not necessary to win outright points with the drop shot. You can often win the point on your next return with a passing shot or lob. Even if your opponent wins the first few points from your drop shot, you are still getting her tired and the tide will turn. Your variety of shots will keep your opponent off guard and thinking about what you will try next. I do not expect you to hit a different shot every time. But mixed in with consistent forehands and backhands, drops and lobs are effective variations. Now let's continue play.*

Raffaella — *Look at that. I hit a good drop shot but you hit another drop shot back to me.*

Nick — *You're darned right. When you hit a drop shot, you must be prepared to come in. I suggest you automatically move in a few steps when executing the drop shot.*

Raffaella — *I'm beginning to understand. But is the drop shot used in doubles?*

Nick — *Be careful. Two opponents are covering the court in doubles. At times, you might catch both of them at the baseline or out of position. You probably won't get as many chances to hit a drop shot in doubles, but when you do, use it.*

Raffaella — *I see some players hit great shots just over the net with lots of underspin.*

Nick — *What you don't see is the number of times they hit the net. It is better to hit a solid drop shot that lets you win the point on your next shot than to lose points trying for outright winners. Remember, drop shots can be safe and damaging. And they count as much as any overhead or forehand smash.*

Conclusion

There are always going to be players who resist using the lob and the drop shot. For whatever reason, they feel the shots are not aggressive tennis. However, my advice is these shots help you win and you would be foolish to ignore them. Effective drop shots will keep aggressive players off balance and that break in stride and concentration is often all it takes to win.

Remember, when you hit the drop shot it does not have to be an outright winner. It might help your confidence if you think of the drop shot as an approach shot which will set up your put-away. Drop shots are hit with the same motion as your groundstrokes, but without quite as much follow-through.

Hold the ball on the racquet as long as possible and open the face slightly on contact. Keep your wrist firm.

When hit properly, the drop shot will help zap your opponent's energy, keep him off balance and set up your passing and lob shots especially on hot, humid days and in the third set.

13

APPROACH SHOTS

Try to recall how many times you've heard your pro, parent, coach, friend, etc., say "Develop groundstrokes. They are the key to the entire game."

I am not agreeing or disagreeing. But I want you to know the results of solid groundstrokes and what you should be trying to accomplish with them: unforced errors and short returns.

Working all those hours during practice and then not capitalizing on short returns during matches means losses. If you don't take advantage of positive situations you're letting your opponent back into the match.

When you have an opponent falling, do not help him to regain balance — until the point is yours.

For the past several months I have been working with Jimmy Arias, making sure he takes advantage of his powerful groundstrokes.

As a junior, Jimmy could win most points from the baseline. However, he has finally learned there are other professionals who also hit well from the baseline. As a result of better competition Jimmy would overhit, trying to win a long rally. But that only causes needless errors.

Finally, Jimmy is beginning to capitalize and move in, forcing opponents to hit passing shots in order to win the point.

Are you one of the many players who hit a well-placed ground-stroke or serve, see the short ball return, which you hit, but then run back to the baseline and start over again? Learn to approach the net on these balls. It may lead you to victory.

Approach Shot

The approach shot is any shot you hit before going to the net. A key factor to the success of this shot is making contact with the ball in the vicinity of the service line.

By hitting the ball at this location, only a few steps remain for you to close into the net to cover the return at a height you can put away.

This shot usually is preceded by:

A.   A good serve forcing a short return.

B.   A well-placed groundstroke forcing a short return.

C.   An opponent trying to bring you into the net.

How to Hit the Approach Shot

Select a short ball. It is important to be very positive on the ball you want to come in on. The quicker you move, the higher you can make contact with the ball and also catch your opponent far out of position.

Run directly toward the ball. Before arriving, take your racquet back with a short backswing. (Having worked with thousands of students, I am positive it requires more time to run forward with your racquet back. If the ball is a few steps away, take your racquet back; but when going from the baseline to the service line, start your preparation of the racquet while moving. Try this yourself or watch good players when they run forward. They can get their racquet back from the forehand side and not lose a step. But if they prepare too soon from the backhand side, they always seem to lose time.)

Slow down to gain body control. Make contact in front of you; and make sure you have the same follow-through as your other strokes.

(NOTE: In the beginner to low intermediate level, students should come to a stop before making contact with the ball.)

I have watched hundreds of advanced players. They never stop but they slow down enough so as not to run through the ball.

Coming to a complete stop after hustling several steps to the ball is difficult. It's also hard to close into the net after the shot. Do not think I'm telling you to run at full steam. Slow down to hit the ball and if you can do it without losing a step, continue on into the net without a complete stop.

Choice of Shot

The height of the ball, point of contact and position of your opponent can determine how the approach shot should be hit.

A. **Underspin.** This shot offers a great deal of control, especially when hit at a low point and lifted up and over the net. It is easier to hit underspin on the backhand side. Of course, this shot requires a long follow-through. Without it the ball will float and have a high bounce.

 When hitting from the forehand side, you might find it difficult to apply underspin and maintain the long follow-through. A few big-time players, headed by Billie Jean King, often hit an inside out (sidespin) approach shot. The ball not only spins but bounces away from the opponent as well.

B. **Topspin.** For gifted players with strong wrist acceleration, topspin is often hit for an approach shot. Ivan Lendl, with his extreme Eastern Backhand grip, can fool an opponent by taking a very low ball and hitting an outright winner.

C. **Flat Drive.** Quite often when a ball is above waist level, I recommend a flat drive. This ball will be very difficult to recover because it will not bounce as high as the topspin approach. Connors hits this the best.

Underspin for Control and Extra Time

There are times you are forced to go to the net sooner than you would like. When a short ball brings you in, remember underspin not only offers control, it will cause the ball to go much deeper and slower to the baseline. The underspin ball will float through the air. Just be sure it skims low when it hits the surface. A high bounce offers the opponent an excellent chance to pass you.

(NOTE: Chip Hooper and Jimmy Arias have been working on this shot. I recommended that Chip go through the ball with a firm wrist and not slow down on contact.)

By the way, this is an excellent approach shot against two-handed players, like Jimmy Connors and Gene Mayer. Borg, however, has a little less trouble because he releases his left hand on contact with low balls.

Where to Hit Approach Shot

A. **Depth and Position.** The key to the approach shot is depth and position. The ball should land three to four feet inside the baseline and the same distance from the singles line.

 Why not make it better? Human beings are subject to

Short Backswing, and firm on contact on this Backhand Underspin approach shot.

error! Any closer to the line and you have very little chance if you mis-hit the ball even slightly. This position will force your opponent to hit the passing shot while running to the side or moving backward. It will be difficult enough.

B.   **Down the Line.** For the most part, the approach shot should go down the line. Why? You can cover your opponent's best returns which are down the line or a crosscourt attempt.

It is difficult for an opponent to run wide to his backhand and whip a short angle crosscourt return. By coming down the line, you force your opponent to make a difficult return or leave you an easy volley.

Vary the approach on occasion just to keep your opponent off-balance and you'll find yourself winning a lot of points at the net.

14

ESSENTIALS TO YOUR GAME

During my clinics or when traveling, I'm often asked one question from both students and fellow coaches:

What do I think is the single most important factor in making a good tennis player?

That question indicates that people are definitely interested in being at the top. To be the best. To be number one!

Usually when people ask the question, they give their own answer in the form of another question:

The serve?

The volley?

The big forehand?

Concentrate on making few unforced errors?

Confidence?

The answer to all of these questions is the same. No.

Quite frankly, it doesn't matter which single element you name, the answer would still be no. There is no one single element which will make a player a winner. In my opinion, there are three key essentials which go into making a player reach maximum potential.

The three essentials are mobility, consistency and accuracy. Without these three essentials you will find it impossible to reach the top of your game, no matter on what level you play.

In the pro ranks, the players that come to mind as perfect examples of these three essentials are Bjorn Borg, Ken Rosewall, Jimmy Connors, Chris Evert Lloyd and Tracy Austin. Each of these players relies on a specific element to achieve success, but all of them have the three essentials which make their games effective.

A cannonball serve is useless without consistency. Devastating forehands are unimportant without mobility. And without accuracy, all shots are just as likely to be losers as winners.

These three elements are the keys to tennis. And like any other area, you can work at improving them. The following points will help you better your game.

I. Mobility

Many athletes are said to be very fast. This may be true, but they add to their speed by **anticipation.**

To some extent certain athletes seem to have a feel for where the ball is going. They seem to know where the batter will hit, where the halfback will run, etc. This instinct helps a great deal. But you can increase your own mobility by applying the following:

A.   **Watch the ball**

Keep your eyes fixed on the ball at all times and try to figure out where it is going to bounce before it hits the surface. The split second you save will allow you to start moving for the ball faster, which will increase your range.

Also, watch the racquet before your opponent makes contact. **High to low,** with face slightly open, probably means an underspin which will result in a low bounce; **low to high** — topspin with a high bounce.

Watch the opponent's position on the court. If you hit a shot down the line to his backhand which pulls him out of position, you should expect a short return. Be ready to hit a crosscourt shot with your opponent running across the entire baseline in pursuit. It will be difficult for him to hit a deep crosscourt shot. Move before the shot to capitalize.

Don't wait until your opponent gets to the ball and makes a weak return just over the net. Don't stand flatfooted behind the baseline. Anticipation will increase your mobility.

B.   **Get your racquet back.**

As you take your first step, your racquet head should start going back into position. Arthur Ashe feels this is the key to meeting the ball in front of you for effective groundstrokes.

C. **Move your feet.**

As soon as you see the flight of the ball and have an idea where it is going, start moving your feet in that direction.

D. **Foot Movement**

Players generally have their hands full just trying to hit the ball, without concern about which foot to move, or whether to take short or long steps. Harold Solomon has excellent foot movement. Yet if you asked him to explain which foot goes first, he would probably not be able to tell you. With top players, foot movement is a natural motion.

However, if a slow start is part of your problem, you can use the following tips:

1. Step toward the ball with the foot farthest from the ball. By making this first step, it is easy to turn your body and take the racquet back at the same time. You can also continue your forward motion without losing a step.

2. **Side steps** — I try to discourage this movement unless very few steps are required. It's difficult to have shoulder rotation when moving sideways over a long distance. Without shoulder rotation, you can't get your racquet head back without sacrificing balance and this is a key to hitting consistently. Running for wide balls, don't try stopping on contact. Take one extra step after your stroke and push off with that leg for a quick start back into position. Recover immediately.

3. **Bouncing — On Tiptoes** — This extra motion is completely unnecessary for good footwork. A three or five set match could be lost because this extra body motion robs you of energy. Players like Bjorn Borg, Ken Rosewall and Jimmy Connors glide to the ball. They do not waste energy by bouncing.

4. **Weight going forward.** Ken Rosewall usually made the shot because his anchor foot and forward motion started at the same time. He kept his weight moving forward which helped give him momentum.

The key to mobility is believing you can reach every ball. Your first step should be positive and quick.

The necessary elements — the eyes, feet and racquet — must react automatically and all together. Plan on giving extra time to this important factor.

When you see someone reach a ball, remember you can do the same thing if you work at it.

II. Consistency

The best way to explaining this element is:

> Be determined to hit the last ball over the net no matter what your opponent returns to you. Be patient and ready to stay on the court as long as is required to win!

I'm not saying it is necessary to stay on the court all day. Don't make an endurance test out of it. But be patient enough to force a weak return or unforced error.

The playing surface will have a great deal to do with how you play your match. Recently I attended tournaments at both Nice and Monte Carlo where I watched the play of my students Jimmy Arias, Pablo Arraya, and Marco Ostaja. The red clay of France forces the big hitters to be patient and consistent and wait for the right time.

Pablo Arraya was down the first set, 5-1, to Pascal Portes. Pablo was slugging each and every ball and making numerous unforced errors. Upon seeing me, he knew immediately to concentrate on consistency, which meant keeping the ball in play. He did exactly that and won the match in two sets.

I then walked over the stadium court to watch Bjorn Borg qualifying against Ostaja. Borg had not lost his ability to be consistent and was accurate as well. His feet moved like a ballerina as he won 6-0, 6-0. In the locker room afterward, my student said he could not believe how the balls kept coming back at him. He said that after awhile he became impatient and tired and tried shots beyond his ability.

After that I watched Jimmy Arias in the second round of qualifying. He had won the first set, but the second was close in the beginning and gradually it began to slip away. Jimmy was becoming impatient on baseline rallies and was not willing to wait for a short ball or for an unforced error.

Finally in the third set, Jimmy put it back together and won 6-4.

We talked in the locker room after the match and he said he felt he could blast his opponent off the court. But there is no way you can blast anyone off the red clay of Europe. You must be determined to hit those extra balls no matter what. That is what is meant by consistency.

III. Accuracy

The last essential to your game may very well be the most crucial. Accuracy is the final piece of the puzzle that will make you a complete player. When you have the ability to spot the ball where you want it, you will always have a chance to win any match you play because there is always the possibility your opponent will lack this vital quality and your opponent's unforced errors are the biggest weapon you can have.

When your feet are always on the move; when you are consistent enough to hit back one more ball than your opponent; and when you can place your shots in certain locations in the court, you will have the complete game.

The key to accuracy is not trying to put the ball on a certain spot. Accuracy in tennis does not mean the same pin-point control that William Tell needed. You're not trying to hit an exact spot.

Accuracy in tennis means hitting for a certain area. That area should be wide enough so that if you mis-hit a little, you will still be in bounds. No players do this better than Borg, Evert Lloyd and Austin.

Players and fans alike always respond when a powerful shot is smashed down the court and it kicks up a white dust cloud from hitting the line. While those shots look impressive and always get the "oohs" and "aahs," if you were to actually chart a complete match you would find the players who keep that close to the line will actually lose far more points than they win.

The type of accuracy you should strive for is when you can be off a little and still fall into the playing area. This flexibility in accuracy will allow you to remain in baseline rallies — where the ball may be traveling in excess of 70 miles-per-hour — and not make an unforced error.

The next time you're watching Borg on television, try to chart his shots. You will notice that most of his returns are three to five feet from the baseline. But his topspin forehands and backhands will be in that area all day long. With that definition of accuracy, he takes a heavy toll on all opponents.

15

SINGLES STRATEGY

In order to win matches, a player must make use of his offensive talents as well as stay even on defensive plays. Within the limit of experience or skill, you must be flexible and determined; consistent and confident.

Once you have mastered the basic strokes of the game and are committed to winning, the next area that will be of concern is the basic strategy of play. From working with so many different students, I've learned that physical ability will cause a lot of variations on the style of play. Yet there are basic rules and facts that are constant. You must become familiar with them if you intend improving your game.

1. Errors Outnumber Outright Winners

More players lose matches because of errors than win because of so many outright winners. A well-planned strategy, therefore, will force your opponent to make errors while cutting down your own risk.

Everyone talks about the big winners that skim the net or land close to the line. But try keeping a chart. You will find most of these balls hit the net or go long. You will also find that groundstrokes landing consistently deep in the backcourt will draw favorable results. Let your opponent please the crowd with hard shots. You stick to safe returns.

2. Keep Balls in Play

Whatever is required, keep the ball in play until your opponent makes an error.

Do not be concerned about classical strokes, perfect balance, pretty clothes, who is looking, etc. Just hit that ball back even when you're off balance.

We often have our students practice a drill to see who can keep the ball in play the longest.

3. Think — Think — Think

Winning requires a game plan that is basic and simple. Keep in mind that your plan must be adjusted if you're losing by a large margin.

Tennis is more than:

A. serve — volley — point

B. receive — hit a winner.

What happens if your first serve is a little off or you're having trouble in breaking serve? You must be ready to stop and rethink what has happened and if necessary to alter your game.

Use your head at all times and your game will improve.

4. Keep Your Ball High and Deep

So often I hear spectators say "Wow! What a shot. It was so close to the net."

Play me that way and be prepared to pay for the balls.

A comment we often use at the Academy is:

"Whatever portion of the court you can see over the net is where your balls should be hit."

From the baseline you can see very little of the court. Balls should be hit high and deep to land within five to eight feet of the baseline. This depth will keep your opponent on the defensive.

LOBS

— — — — — — — — — — —

6 FT. GROUNDSTROKES

— — — — — — — — — — —

3 FT. APPROACH   PUTAWAY

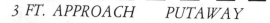

Hit your ground strokes high and deep.

Balls should clear the net with a rainbow arc (five to eight feet). That's right, not five to eight inches, but five to eight feet!

When getting closer to the net, you can observe more of the opponent's court and that's the time to angle your shots.

5. Get Your First Serve In

I often make our students play with one serve. It is imperative to get your first serve in as often as possible because:

A.   Opponents are not usually prepared to attack first serves.

B.   The pressure of putting your second serve in play will result in defensive serves.

Remember, power is not always the key to a successful first serve. Positioning the ball with controlled spin will do just as much as a bouncing first serve.

6. Serve — Volley

Unless playing on an extremely slow surface or facing a Rod Laver or Jimmy Connors, try to serve and volley whenever possible. When forced to stay back, try to get to the net as quickly as possible.

7. Attack Short Balls on First Opportunity

On the very first short ball, you must attack! Do not stay back. If your opponent is hitting short balls as a result of your well-placed deep groundstrokes, you must take advantage of it.

Attack when you get a ball in your offensive zone.

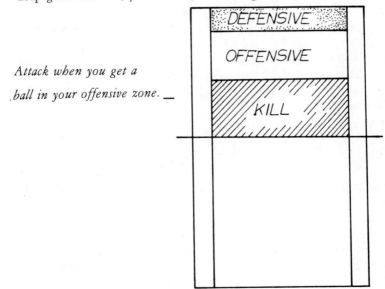

Capitalize on the **very first** opportunity. You may not get another. You will soon learn the correct time to attack. But I would rather have you come in too often and work backwards than to come in once a set.

8. In Trouble, In Doubt — Go Crosscourt

Whenever you are in doubt, go crosscourt. By hitting crosscourt, you meet the ball in front of you and it travels the longest distance on the court, allowing you extra room for an error and time to recover.

Also most players feel more comfortable hitting crosscourts than they do pushing down the line. Hitting crosscourt means crossing the net at the lowest point and returning in the same direction so it requires very little adjustment on your part.

(NOTE: At times, I urge students to alter this strategy and to go down the line because it keeps opponents off balance and makes your crosscourts more effective. It would be wise to practice both shots, but concentrate on the crosscourt because it is the best safety valve.)

Remember to stay with your down-the-line shots and hit them in the same manner as a crosscourt, perhaps just a little later.

9. Strengths and Weaknesses

You must understand the strengths and weaknesses of your own game as well as those of your opponents.

Maximize your strong points to offset your weak points. Maintaining control of the ball will make it more difficult for your opponent to get to your weakness.

In warm-up, deliberately hit your weak shots. Who knows, you may hit a few so well that your opponent might think he was playing your strong shots. This will cause confusion and doubt that should help you.

Once the match begins, take advantage of shots you can hit offensively. Never wait for another chance.

If your opponent has an obvious weakness, go after it. Not only will he make errors, but he will be off balance when you hit to his strong shots.

10. Return of Serve

In the beginning, get that return back in play. After you build confidence and you can apply additional pressure without making unforced errors — do it. (See chapter on return of serve.)

11. Steady Player — Bring Him In
Volleyer — Keep Him Back

Do the opposite of whatever your opponent is most comfortable with:

A. Baseliner — Hit short underspins to service line area, drop shots, etc. Bring him in. Pass or lob him!

B. Volleyer.
1. Hit high looping, deep groundstrokes.
2. When in trouble, hit high defensive lobs.
3. Get your first serve in.
4. Keep opponent off balance by moving him side to side.

C. Hard Hitter — Change the pace at all times. Concede he is more powerful and hit a wide variety of balls to throw off his timing.

D. Pusher — Do not become impatient and try to blow him off the court. Be patient and stay with him until he makes an error. Do not be hesitant in bringing him in and go in on any short ball he gives you. Do not get discouraged if he wins the first few points while you're putting your game plan into action.

12. Spin with Spin

Students have most difficulty with spin balls (underspin, topspin) by trying to hit them too hard with a different type of shot. I suggest:

A. Underspin with underspin.

B. Topspin with topspin.

C. Topspin with underspin.

D. Underspin with topspin. (with C and D concentrate to a higher degree when changing action on a ball)

E. Underspin — low to high with a firm wrist. Do not try to put the ball away.

13. Adjust for Court Surfaces — Playing Surfaces

Playing surfaces will dictate your type of play. It is imperative you realize and accept what can and cannot be accomplished and stay within that framework so the percentages will be in your favor.

A. **European Red Clay**

Be prepared to stay on the court all day to win one point. You cannot blast consistent winners from the baseline without numerous errors. You must have patience and wait until a short ball or error comes about. Placement of serves far outweighs an infrequent ace. Be sure to get your first serve in or expect being attacked on the second serve. Touch, drop shots and high deep balls are part of this game. Do not come in too often on second serves or weak approach shots. Be ready to stay out there. The 1982 French Open Championship took five hours with fifty ball rallies.

B. **Cement, Grass, Indoor Carpet**
   1. Serve and volley usually determine the point.
   2. Be sure to have an excellent first volley.
   3. Well-placed groundstrokes with topspin from both sides are important.

C. **Sun, Wind, Heat, Poor Background**
   The wind can be a major asset if used correctly.
   1. Hitting into the wind — Make sure your balls are hit hard, high and deep. Get into the net on your first short ball. Use a little more spin on first serve.
   2. Hitting with the wind — For control use lots of topspin, making sure balls land between service line and baseline. Attack at all times. Never give up control of the ball.
   3. Strong crosswinds — Hit most of your balls down the center when in trouble or crosscourt away from the wind. Do not lob or push a ball down the line in the direction the wind is blowing.

14. Strategy

A. If winning, do not change your tactics.
B. If behind, try to analyze what change should be made.
C. Learn how to play crucial points and games.
D. Do not let a bad call or your opponent's game tactics break your concentration.
E. Remember the opponent is just as nervous as you.
F. Do not guide the ball when nervous. Let the racquet do the work and use long follow-throughs.
G. Hit deep, serve deep, and hit hard when you begin to tighten.

16

DOUBLES STRATEGY

Singles play requires concentration on the ball and your opponent and is played with a higher note of competition. There is no partner to provide help. You must accept the win or loss on your own merit.

Doubles has more variables. You must still be ready to play, but you must also know the basic differences when playing a doubles match. Not only does strategy differ in doubles play, but certain styles seem to lend themselves to doubles better than others:

A. Excellent Singles and Doubles
    Brian Gottfried and Raul Ramirez
B. Excellent Doubles
    Stan Smith and Bob Lutz
C. Excellent Singles
    Stan Smith
D. Good Singles
    Bob Lutz
E. Excellent Doubles — Good Singles
    Frew McMillan and Bob Hewitt
F. Excellent Doubles — Fair Singles
    Freddy McNair, Sherwood Stewart, Ferdi Taylan

Throughout this chapter I will outline and discuss the differences in singles and doubles play and offer tips that will help you capitalize on your strong and weak points as well as those of your partner and exploit the weaknesses of your opponents.

1. Doubles As A Team Sport

Team sports require athletes who know and respect each other. It is important to accept your partner and work within his or her capabilities rather than wishing he could do something different. Remember to concentrate on your partner's positive points instead of getting upset by the negative.

Doubles is a team game.

A doubles team should capitalize on their strengths, realize and accept their weaknesses and try to protect themselves whenever exploited. Not only do you play your game as a team, but you must break down your opponents with a very careful game plan.

Make sure your personalities do not clash and be prepared to swallow your ego if your opponents can do a little more. The scoreboard does not say whether your partner is stronger or weaker than you. Only results are posted. If you are capable of doing two or three shots extremely well and your partner four or five, make sure you work to take advantage of this. You are a team, and must work together to be most effective.

2. Conversation With Your Partner

Too many people keep problems, questions and answers within themselves. They want to speak up and express their viewpoints but say nothing because they worry about offending the partner.

This silence does nothing but maximize the problem. When playing doubles you must discuss certain situations with your partner:

    A.   If having trouble returning first serve, tell your partner and work out your best defense.

    B.   If nervous and somewhat tight on your serve or overhead, talk about it.

C. Having trouble recovering a lob or hitting an overhead, talk about it.

Learn to compliment your partner and give encouragement after an error. When changing sides, exchange viewpoints on weaknesses or strengths in your game as well as your opponents'.

3. Poach — Error! Keep Practicing!

Too many players are determined to defend the net, especially on a weak return, and are always eager to poach when playing doubles.

On your very first attempt to poach, suppose you miss a set-up. Do you fall into the category of never moving again for the remaining part of the match? Does your partner say, "How in the world did you miss that ball?"

Try to remember these tips:

A. Make a decision to poach before the opponent hits the ball on return of serve. This gives you time to reach the ball and alerts your partner to switch sides. This, also, applies to poaching during rallies. If you wait too long, both you and your partner will end up in an I formation and unable to cover the return. If you attempt a poach without warning your partner, make sure it is a winner.

B. Poaching applies pressure and keeps your opponents on edge. Even if you miss the poach, you have accomplished part of your strategy which could cause unforced errors at a later time.

C. Try to analyze your opponents' style of play. If they hit the same shots most of the time, it makes it easy to poach.

D. Some effective doubles teams use signals with each other when getting ready to poach, especially on return of serve.

E. Try moving forward when poaching. This will help you cut the ball off sooner and improve on the effectiveness of the poach.

Don't be afraid to poach. It is the winning way.

4. Serve — First — Second Position

Aces are far less important in doubles so your big serve is far less effective. The name of the game is to get your first serve in most of the time and apply spin and accuracy on your second which will permit you to come in and not have a ball slammed back at your ankles.

Serving down the middle of the court cuts the angle of return to either the middle or crosscourt. This gives the serving team an excellent chance to cover the return.

When the receiving team makes an adjustment to cover the return, you should serve wide, taking them off the court. When your partner sees the receiver going wide, he should move to the alley to protect against the return.

Powerful, flat serves cut down your time to move in close for the return. Spin serves will give you an extra step or two and also put the receiver off balance for the return.

5. Take Over the Net (King of the Hill)

When we were youngsters we played "King of the Hill." Whoever took over the hill seemed to have a psychological edge and won most of the time. This principle applies to taking the net on your very first opportunity.

A. Serve and move in.
B. Move in on short groundstroke returns.
C. Attack a vulnerable serve.

The best combinations in doubles are:

A. Two up.
B. Two back.
C. One up — one back.

It is better to come in too soon than to stay back and give up net control.

6. First Volley

As mentioned in the chapter on first volleys, this shot often determines the outcome of the point.

But the position of the first volley is somewhat different in doubles.

Singles — Deep down the line. Protect that side for the return because hitter must cover the entire court and is often late or off balance when hitting the return down the line.

Doubles — The first volley should go deep to the center most of the time, unless your opponents are out of position or you want to keep them honest by going down the line or crosscourt.

Hitting deep down the center gives you time to position yourself opposite your partner and prepare for the return.

Hitting down the middle also cuts down the angle for passing shots.

7. Protect and Defend Against the Lob

There are a few suggestions that might help you against the lob.

A. Do not fear the lob. Go after the ball as if you own it.

B. Protect your side of the court. If unable to reach the ball, react quickly by telling your partner.

C. Try to hit overhead without a bounce.

D. A lob hit within the service line area should be smashed and you should move back into the net. Your partner should hold his position.

If the lob is deep and near the baseline area, your partner should retreat at the very same time. Try to work your way back to the net as quickly as possible.

Let your partner return the Deep Lob over your head.

8. When in Doubt — Hit Down the Center

Not only are you hitting the ball over the net at the lowest height, but it will cause confusion to the opponents as they decide who should hit the ball.

9. Both Players at Net — Who Hits the Volley

Quite often when a good approach shot or volley is hit by your opponent, you and your partner are both in position to hit the return. But there can be hesitation as to who should hit the ball. This loses the offensive advantage. The rule of thumb is:

The player who hit the last ball should take the return. He knows where he hit his shot and can anticipate where the return might come from. Or the player with the stronger stroke should take the ball. Work with your partner to decide which way is best for you.

125

10. Aim Your Groundstroke or Exchange Volley
at Opponent's Right Hip

It is very difficult to play a ball hit directly at your right hip. You will be too close to the ball to attempt a forehand volley, unless the ball was hit with no pace.

Sliding the racquet across your body and hitting a backhand block volley will get the ball back, but only defensively.

11. Watching the Ball Only — Not Good Enough

Not only must a good doubles player watch the ball, but he must have some concept or feeling of:

A. Partner's position.
B. Watching the receiver.
C. Watching receiver's position.
D. Watching the ball.

All of the above play an important role in your position and your next move. The following game situations illustrate how you must consider all the elements:

A. An effective lob has been hit over your partner's head. In fact, it is so good he has to scramble to get it on a bounce. With this in mind, start moving back at the very same time.

B. Your partner is able to drive the volley down at your opponent's feet. Be ready to poach when the opponent has to hit up on the ball.

C. Your partner hits an effective offensive return of the second serve. You should be ready to move in to the net and cut off the defensive return.

12. No-No Shots and Their Corrections

Keep in mind that certain shots have a very low percentage and should not be tried too often.

1. **No-No:** Cannonball serves.
   Correction: A well-placed first serve with a little spin for control. Keep the receiver off balance with most serves down the middle. But occasionally hit wide balls or jam the receiver.

2. **No-No:** Push second serve and come to the net.
   Correction: A consistent second serve, but with confidence, spin and full extension.

3. **No-No:** Outright winners on return of serve.
   Correction: Hit a consistent crosscourt return of serve landing in the area of the service line. Vary this with

an occasional lob or go down the line to keep
the server's partner honest.

4.   **No-No:**   Winning first volleys.

    Correction: Errors will outnumber outright first volley win-
ners. Place the ball deep with the majority go-
ing down the center.

5.   **No-No:**   Feeble overheads.

    Correction: An overhead should be hit offensively, especially
when you're pulled out of position. Hitting easy
overheads will let your opponents off the hook
and they may get you out of position, opening
a large area between you and your partner.

6.   **No-No:**   Winning overheads from behind the baseline.

    Correction: Hitting winning overheads from the baseline is
very difficult because your opponents have had
time to regain their positions. The ball must
travel approximately eighty feet, losing its offensive punch. You are better off hitting up on
the ball, guaranteeing depth, which will make
it an offensive shot.

7.   **No-No:**   Numerous drop shots, especially on hard courts.

    Correction: The position of two opponents with at least one
playing fairly close to the net places the drop
shot in the low percentage group. At times you
may get both opponents in the back court while
you're fairly close to the net. Then a drop shot
is effective.

8.   **No-No:**   Hitting a short-angle volley when large openings are available.

    Correction: Do not hit cute shots when large openings are
available. Hitting drop volleys and cuties will
backfire.

9.   **No-No:**   Hitting numerous shots down the line.

    Correction: Trying to hit down the line is a stupid shot. It
should be tried every so often to prevent cons-
tant poaching and to prove you can do it. But
don't let your urge for passing shots force you
into careless errors.

10.   **No-No:**   Hitting more than an occasional half-volley.

    Correction: Half-volleys in doubles will be destructive. Try
to get that extra step into the net so you can
volley. Do not be frightened or stop on the ser-

vice line as if it were a magnet. Move in as quickly as possible.

11.   **No-No:**   Always having to hit up on your volleys.

     Correction: Always having to hit up on your volley could mean: you're too slow moving in; too frightened to move in close; or your serve, groundstrokes and volleys should be improved.

12.   **No-No:**   Always trying to drive through the opponents when positioned close to the net.

     Correction: Driving through the opponents all the time will force them to be ready. Mix up your shots with lobs and chips.

13.   **No-No:**   Failure to utilize the lob.

     Correction: The lob is and always will remain a weapon. Be proud and willing to lob. The lob makes the net rusher a little more hesitant and anything which throws your opponent off balance should be used.

13. Doubles Tips

A.   Which Partner To Serve First

1.   The strong server should be first up. There is no better strategy than to win the first game.

2.   Be sure to get the first serve in. Serve down the middle but also use variation.

3.   Partners should poach at times to cause concern to their opponents. But do not poach all the time. A simple signal to the server is a good idea.

4.   If receiver is constantly putting pressure on server, use the Australian formation — stay back at times.

Australian Formation puts pressure on a good crosscourt return of serve.

B. Receiving

1. Partners should discuss what side they feel most secure with.

2. Getting the ball back in play is important, but more pressure must be applied. Move inside the baseline or favor your strong side when returning. Remember, your partner is taking care of half of the court so you can be a little more out of position when receiving service.

3. The safest return is the crosscourt. Keep this in mind and try to angle the ball to bounce close to where the singles sideline and service line bisect. This forces the server to move laterally for volley and to get down to the ball. This type of return should produce defensive volleys or errors.

4. Keep the net man honest with an occasional ball down the line or directly at them. You may not win the point, but it will alert them that you can do it!

5. Do not be hesitant to use the good old reliable lob. This shot should be defensive most of the time, unless you can control the serve and hit an offensive lob. Lobbing will often slow down the attacking server, especially if his partner is having trouble with his overhead.

6. Try to vary your return to keep opponents off balance.

7. Try to keep the pressure on them at all times. Hit with confidence and remember topspin groundstrokes will drop very quickly making the ball more difficult to volley.

17

PLAYING CRUCIAL POINTS

For the most part players do not give enough thought to the crucial points of a game or a match. Even some of the best players never truly think a game through. They play each point the same, ignoring the very important fact that during a match there are very likely to be important points that will make the difference.

How often have we all heard players say:

"I had them down 40-0, or 5-2, and then they got lucky and wound up beating me"?

What they don't consider is that they might have lost the key points. These points are the turning points upon which the outcome of the match will pivot. When you win the big points, you do more than enhance your score. You get a big psychological boost as well.

There is no way to calculate the effect of having a reputation of winning most of the big points. But if you have that edge, the pressure is certainly on your opponent. In order to be most effective, you must know how to select the big points of a game and the crucial games of a match and how to win them.

Learn From The Master

The name Bjorn Borg is always part of the conversation when the match is down to the wire. Borg does not get upset or visually nervous when involved in a tie-breaker or when playing a big point. He does not crack if:

(A) close calls go against him, (B), net calls go against him, or (C) the ball hits a line and skids.

Instead he will tighten his belt, play exactly like his entire match and take advantage of the very first opportunity to win the point.

He may strive to add just a little more on all his shots, but he will not take wild chances.

Serving — Your Lead

The fourth point of any game is the crucial point to win. Examples:

A. Serving — 30-15, win — 40-15

Being up by two points is a substantial lead that gives you confidence and places the opponent in a very vulnerable position. He must win the next two points.

B. Serving — 30-15, lose — 30-30

You find yourself tied knowing this should not be the score on your service. You begin to tighten a little which gives the opponent that little opening to break serve. Instead, take a moment at 30-15 and think how you played the previous point. Do not change your tactics if you won the previous point. If you lost it, make sure the error is not repeated.

If your opponent won it on a low percentage shot, continue your style of play. Be sure to get the first serve in by taking a little speed off and adding a spin slice to your ball. But do not change your game.

At 40-0, go for broke! This does not mean to hit an impossible shot, but:

1. Try for an ace.
2. Run around a short return and hit that big forehand.
3. Serve and volley.
4. Take advantage of the first opportunity. In fact, gamble a little. Come in on a deeper ball than you normally would.

Returning Serve

GET THE FIRST POINT! — GET THE FIRST POINT!

Roscoe Tanner would be a bit unnerved to think he lost his first point in spite of his cannonball serve. Remember, all the books and coaches preach and players feel they are at a disadvantage when receiving service. Make a firm stance of this negative situation. Knowing you are at a disadvantage, take the "What the heck attitude." Unleash your forehand down the line.

If it works, try again. If it works again, pinch yourself and wake up. This time change that big return to a safe lob or attack the serve. This will really cause confusion and who knows, you may break serve!

Break Point — Receiving Service (Your AD)

At this point, the server is really thinking what to do with his first serve. John Newcombe was at his best receiving serves at this point. He would actually stand in the doubles alley letting you know his forehand return was coming, and he intended to use it right now. He was not bashful! He was bold!

The server fully knew the position he was in and usually was determined to hit a big one down the center. I guarantee Newcombe did not have to hit that big forehand all the time. There were many double faults. Jimmy Arias, a present student, just waits for the same opportunity. At that point, the receiving player has a psychological advantage. Use it with confidence. Go for the winner and dare your opponent.

Seventh Game — Often Decides Match

There are several situations a set could be in at this game: 4-2, 5-1, 6-0, but the game is crucial if the score is 3-all.

No matter what, win this game at all costs. This same attitude applies to serving or returning serve at this time. Do not tighten up. Reach up for that serve and, of course, get it in by adding a bit more spin. Don't dare risk the second serve. The opponent will attack. Remember the simple solution to the serve. Hit up and out with full extension and spin for control. Go for this point.

Do You Fear Set or Match Point?

Ending a match is often like signing the papers for your first new car. You do not believe it's over until you are holding the trophy or driving down the street.

But to complete this step requires planning and understanding of what was needed to do it. Quite often, players will panic at this point and play the point without any thought, hoping and praying the opponent will make an error.

You must remember the opponent is fighting for his life and will do anything to stay in the match. Take a second to calm yourself and remember three things:

1. Get your first serve in.
2. Return service.

3.   Try to execute the shot in which you have the most confidence.

To have reached set or match point means you have done well to this point. Do not make any major changes. Calm yourself and rethink all the points you have won. Concentrate on your positive shots. Remember you reached match point so you need play no differently to win it all!

18

HOW TO PRACTICE

Once all the strokes are learned, practice is the key to performing well in match play. Proper practice will enhance a player's chances of reaching his full potential.

A case in point is Chip Hooper. Chip is a gifted athlete. Yet with all his talent, it took total dedication and a strict practice schedule to help him develop into a top player. Chip Hooper combined match play, practice sets, rigorous drills, footwork, and great mental attitude to become the player he is today. Of all his practice habits, nothing impressed us more than the concentration he put into the drills. It is repetitive drilling that gives the muscle the memory to perform during match play.

For novice players, improvement takes time. It took time for a great natural athlete like Chip. Chip was advised by Arthur Ashe and his college coach, Tom Pucci, both close personal friends, to take a semester off from school to work on his game diligently. It took four months, but when Chip Hooper returned to college, he won the NCAA indoor championship. He has since gone on to success on the men's professional tour. Remember, to be the best or even to improve, takes time. Practice time, if used wisely, can help you reach new plateaus.

(NOTE: Nov. 15, 1981 Chip Hooper returned to the Academy recuperating from an operation on both eyes. He was discouraged and lacked confidence. We sat and discussed his long-range goals to make it big! The blue prints were decided with all tournament planning being handled by Pro Serve with Peter Lawler and Bill Shelton handling all details. Jan. 18, 1982 Chip left the Academy with a ranking of 248. The boom started at the National Indoors and it continued. Within four months he broke into the top twenty. Ability, discipline, and dedication along with hundreds of hours of drilling helped Chip accomplish his goal. We at the Academy are proud of his achievements.)

Group drills help perfect stroke mechanics.

19

DISCIPLINED PRACTICE

1. The Importance of Practice

The very next time you're waiting for a court, observe the players who are rallying and the manner in which they are attempting to practice.

I will wager that you will observe some or all of the following:

1. Balls bouncing several times before player makes contact.
2. Players apologizing when hitting balls away from the opponent.
3. Players discussing the previous night's activities.
4. Rallying without any plan.

This practice pattern will do very little for your game.

I firmly believe that practice habits overlap to form actual playing habits.

It is essential to utilize your practice sessions in the most constructive manner!

2. Pre-Warm-Up Exercise

Quite often you will have to wait before a court is available.

Use this time, even if courts are available, by doing a few warm-up exercises.

Currently, I am involved with the Sports Rehabilitation Institute which has developed a physical fitness program. So many injuries can be prevented by loosening up your body before attempting 100 mile-per-hour serves, overheads or quick starts for wide balls. It is essential to warm up properly.

(NOTE: A chapter on this subject is included in this book.)

3. Do You Practice Your Strengths or Weaknesses or Everything?

My mind often drifts back to my good old high school days. My Dad would ask me if I did my homework, especially math. My answer would always be the same: "It's all done."

The truth of the matter was that everything was done, except for math. I flunked it twice and only passed it on the third attempt because I was on the football team!

If I had to do it over again, my game plan would be:
A.   I would not hide the math book, but I would acknowledge difficulty.
B.   I would ask for extra help.
C.   I would practice my math at the very beginning of every study session.

It is essential to know and accept what you do real well, fair, and not so good!

You are fortunate because you have an opportunity to overcome your weak points with a constructive plan.

While you concentrate on your weak spots, do not take your positive points for granted. Work to improve them also.

4. Lubricate The Engine — Start Slow

At the very beginning of your practice session, do not overhit any strokes.

Be loose and relaxed. Concentrate on a pre-game warm-up before you start serious exercise.

5. Practice Session — A Total Plan

Practice sessions should include:
A.   Pre-warm-up.
B.   Work on weak and strong points.
C.   Try shots you would attempt in a match.
D.   Do not be too loose or try to impress spectators.
E.   Extend yourself the very same way you would if you were playing the biggest match of your career.
F.   Your practice session should vary from stroke production speed drills to actual game type play.

Practice the way you plan to play. I feel all players would improve if they maintain sound practice suggestions.

Practice Drills

Once you have committed yourself to serious practice and are prepared mentally for improving your game, you must have a blueprint from which to construct your new skills.

At the Academy, we use a plan which includes basic drills. These drills are designed to force students to practice definite areas of their game. By incorporating these drills into your practice regimen, you'll be sharpening playing skills and getting the most effective use of the time you spend on the court.

The following are the drills used at the Academy:

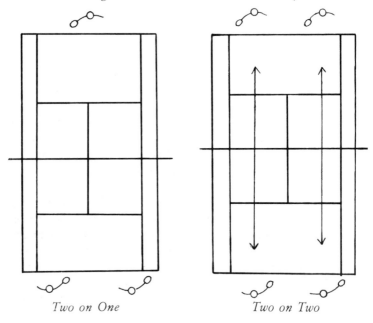

Two on One   *Two on Two*

1. Two on one from the baseline
   OBJECTIVE: To improve consistency and mobility.
   OPERATION: Two players on baseline keep ball in play and move the single player side to side.

2. Two on two from the baseline
   OBJECTIVE: Develop control and consistency.
   OPERATION: Players on baselines hit down the lines and then crosscourts.

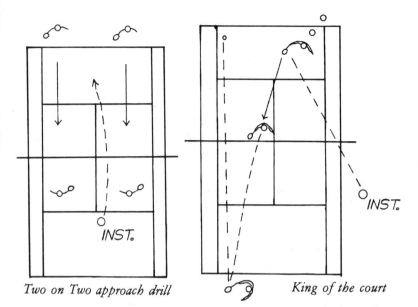

Two on Two approach drill   *King of the court*

3. Two on two approach and come in and play out the volley.
    OBJECTIVE: Sharpen reflexes and approach shots.
    OPERATION: Two players of one team at net. Opposing team on baseline. Ball is put into play by instructor. Baseline team approaches and plays out point.
4. King of the court
    OBJECTIVE: Sharpen volleys and passing shots.
    OPERATION: One player (A) waits on baseline as does opponent (B). Player (B) hits approach and comes to net. (A) tries to pass (B) at net. After point is over (C) takes (B) place. Rotation continues until (B) or (C) wins five points from (A). (B) or (C) then takes (A) place.
5. Around the world
    OBJECTIVE: Develop down the line shots and controlled volleys.
    OPERATION: Used for four or more (plus coach) players. (A) hits down the line to (B) who volleys down the line. Second ball fed crosscourt. (A) again hits down the line to (B) and (B) volleys down the line. Repeat four or five times, then rotate players.

6. Forehand weapon development

OBJECTIVE: To develop forehand into a weapon by forcing student to run around backhand on short balls.

OPERATION: Used with two or more players and a coach. Ball is fed short and high to backhand side. Player runs around backhand and hits offensive forehand. Player then follows shot into the net for volley.

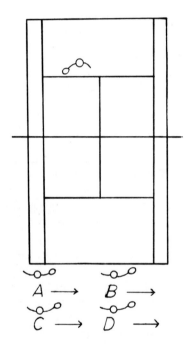

Windshield wiper

7. Windshield Wiper

OBJECTIVE: Improve groundstrokes, footwork or volleys.

OPERATION: 1.) Feeder stands at service line. Players stand on baseline. Player (A) and (B) are 10 feet apart on baseline.

2.) Feeder hits ball wide to (A) so he moves to hit groundstroke. At the same time (B) slides across to the center line and shadow-hits a stroke at the same time (A) is making contact with the ball. The feeder hits

a ball to (B) wide. (B) moves wide to hit
the shot and (A) recovers and shadows a
stroke.

3.) Pattern continues until feeder rotates
players.

8.   Dink Game
     OBJECTIVE: Learn to control racquet face. Work on
                 angles and drop shots.
     OPERATION: Players stand on service lines and hit the
                 ball back and forth. Make sure ball bounces
                 in front of your opponent so you can work
                 on racquet control.

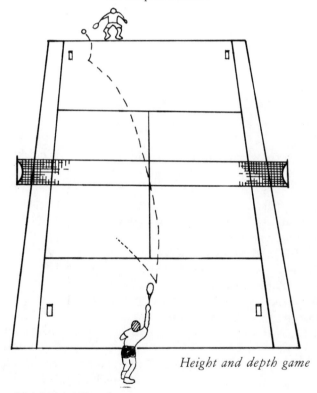

Height and depth game

9.   Height and Depth
     OBJECTIVE: To keep the ball in opponent's backcourt
                 by hitting ball high above the net.
     OPERATION: Place targets six feet from baseline. Play out
                 points until opponent hits ball short of
                 target. Games can be played to twenty-one.

20

PHYSICAL CONDITIONING

Watching tournaments throughout the world, it quickly becomes evident the difference between two otherwise equal players is usually conditioning. Conditioning — defined as physical strength, stamina, power, balance, and speed — is everything when tennis skills are equally balanced. Conditioning is essential, but to condition properly takes good planning, patience and a structured work-out program.

To improve the conditioning program at the Tennis Academy, we associated ourselves with the Sports Performance and Rehabilitation Institute (SPRI). Not only does the SPRI conditioning program improve the physical strength, power, stamina, balance and speed of the students, it also helps prevent injuries common to the game (tennis elbow, ankle sprains, bad shoulders) by strengthening injury-prone areas.

Our conditioning program is simple and effective. It combines footwork, calisthenics (emphasis on the core muscles), jogging, weight training, exercises using rubber bands for resistance and the Nick Bollettieri Tennis Handle (stroke simulation) to develop a well-conditioned, less injury-prone player. Traditionally, tennis has been a sport requiring development of certain skills such as shot placement, stroke production, and footwork. In fact, the major part of this book has been devoted to these topics.

Jogging, developing stamina

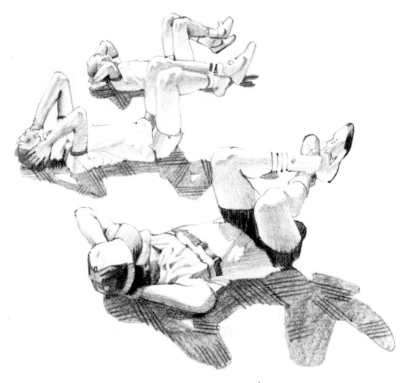

Sit ups, works core muscles

Push ups, develops upper body

But tennis has been evolving along the same lines as volleyball. A clear distinction is now made between recreational volleyball and "power volleyball." Tennis, as it is played at the competitive level, could accurately be labeled "power tennis." It certainly is not the game played years ago. The physical demands of the stops and starts, the sprints forward and backward and the cutting left and right place incredible strain on joints and muscles. These movements must be repeated again and again, with only a few seconds rest between efforts.

Then, too, a player must deal with environmental stresses — weather conditions that range from extreme heat, with its subsequent dehydration to bone-chilling cold with its attendant muscle spasms and cramps. Then there are surface conditions that increase the chance of injury, including slippery grass and clay and the unforgiving nature of hard courts which exact a toll on the joints. When you add the varying demands on agility and timing often stretched to the limits from gusting winds, blankets of fog or vision-blurring sunlight, these factors combine to test the maximum psychological and physical performance of the athlete.

It is a natural law that energy is finite and will run out at some point. Yet the tennis player cannot be concerned with conservation to make sure he can last the match. So the central issue of physical training for tennis is to become more efficient — to learn how to use the appropriate amount of energy at the appropriate time (never too much or too little). In other words, you have to know when to spend energy and know how to do it. The well-conditioned tennis player should move with the speed, accuracy, and explosive power of a panther rather than with the endurance of a mule. That player must also possess enough reserve energy to repair minor damage and recover totally to be physically ready again the next day.

All components of fitness are incorporated here in a unique training program combining solid principles from the sciences of physical education and biomechanics. The training program has been designed specifically so the tennis player can prevent injuries and improve performance and has been used successfully by pros such as John McEnroe and Andrea Jaeger. Whether you are a professional, junior player or weekend athlete, this program will help you meet these two vital goals: playing better tennis and avoiding injuries.

Lower Extremity Training

The POWERBRAND is a natural gum rubber band that can be used for a comprehensive exercise program for the lower body. The POWERBANDs come in assorted widths; the wider the POWERBAND the more resistance is exerted. POWERBAND exercises are excellent for athletes of all ages and abilities and are equally valuable in rehabilitation, injury prevention and conditioning.

Throughout the exercise descriptions you will be instructed to do the following:

1. Strength — a slow steady, sustained movement with a static point of "hold" at the end. The return from the end "hold" is also slow, steady and sustained. Remember, slow and controlled for each of three strength movements.

2. Stamina — a quick "flick" movement done only at the last few degrees of the strength movement. The stamina of "terminal flicks" are done twenty-five times.

3. Power — an explosive movement from start to end with a "hold" at the end point. The return is slow, steady, and sustained. Remember, explode; hold; slow return for three repetitions.

Proper body position is important in performing these exercises. Perfect skeletal alignment should be maintained with the abdominal muscles tight and firm and the spine in a long line.

As you become stronger your program can be altered as follows:

1. Do more repetitions of Strength, Stamina, and Power.

2. Position the POWERBAND farther away from the joint being worked.

3. Use a wider POWERBAND or use more than one POWERBAND.

4. Go through the series of exercises more than once (circuits).

Your POWERBAND program should be done three times per week on alternate days.

The support system described is a nylon strap made to fit in a door or around a secured object. You may use a belt or dog collar secured to furniture in place of the support system.

DORSIFLEXION

Placement of Support System: Bottom of door.

Placement of POWERBAND: Around right forefoot.

Starting Position: Legs straight out — foot in line with the support system.

Action: Slowly, pull your toes back as far as possible.

Repetitions: 10 Strength; 25 Stamina; Repeat for left foot.

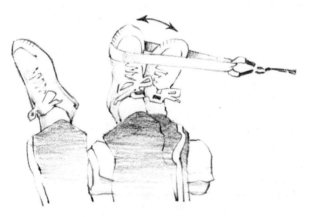

INVERSION

Placement of Support System: Side of door, forefoot height.

Placement of POWERBAND: Around forefoot at right angle to support system.

Starting Position: Sitting with legs straight out, right side to support system, POWERBAND held taut against the inside edge of the foot.

Action: Slowly, turn foot inward, keeping the foot upright (dorsiflexed).

Repetitions: 10 Strength; 25 Stamina; Repeat for left foot.

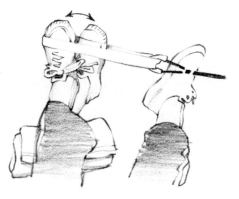

EVERSION

Placement of Support System: Side of door, forefoot height.

Placement of POWERBAND: Around forefoot at right angle to the support system.

Starting Position: Sitting with legs straight out, right side to support system, POWERBAND held taut against the inside edge of the foot.

Action: Slowly, turn foot inward, keeping the foot upright (dorsiflexed).

Repetitions: 10 Strength; 25 Stamina; Repeat for left foot.

HIP FLEXION (Straight Leg Raise)

Placement of Support System: Not needed.

Placement of POWERBAND: Around both legs above the knees.

Starting Position: Lying on back, with both legs straight out in front, small of back pressed flat to floor.

Action: Tighten thigh muscles (push knee cap down) slowly raise right leg keeping both knees locked.

Repetitions: 3 Strength; 25 Stamina; 3 Power; Repeat for left leg.

HIP HYPEREXTENSION (Straight Leg Raise — Back)
Placement of Support System: Not needed.
Placement of POWERBAND: Place POWERBAND around both legs above the knee.
Starting Position: Lying on stomach, forehead on the floor in hands, pressing the hips against the floor.
Action: Slowly, raise right leg as high as possible, keeping the right hip in contact with the floor.
Repetitions: 3 Strength; 25 Stamina; 3 Power; Repeat for left leg.

HIP ABDUCTION (Straight Leg Raise To Side)
Placement of Support System: Not needed.
Placement of POWERBAND: Place POWERBAND around both legs above the knees.
Starting Position: Lying on left side, right leg on top, with body in a straight line, keeping the hips rolled forward and supporting yourself with the right hand.
Action: Lock the right knee back, slowly raise leg — Don't swing leg forward or back, but raise in a straight line.
Repetitions: 3 Strength; 25 Stamina; 3 Power; Repeat for left leg.

149

HIP ADDUCTION (Straight Leg Pull Toward Center)

Placement of Support System: Bottom of door.

Placement of POWERBAND: Around right ankle.

Starting Position: Sitting with both legs straight out, and apart, right side to support system, with POWERBAND taut against inside of right ankle.

Action: Slowly pull right leg toward center of body.

Repetitions: 3 Strength; 25 Stamina; 3 Power; Repeat for left leg.

KNEE FLEXION

Placement of Support System: Not needed.

Placement of POWERBAND: Around both legs at ankle.

Starting Position: Lie face down on floor, both legs straight out, keep your forehead and hips on the floor.

Action: Slowly bend right leg up as far as possible, keeping the left leg straight.

Repetitions: 3 Strength; 25 Stamina; 3 Power; Repeat for left leg.

UPPER EXTREMITY TRAINING

The Nick Bollettieri Tennis Handle is used for strength and injury prevention for the arm; shoulder; and elbow.

Your TENNIS HANDLE exercises should be done three times per week on alternate days. As described in the POWERBAND exercises, you will perform strength and stamina movements only.

In performing these exercises, the tension on the tubing should be such that all movements can be performed through a **full** range of motion. If you cannot reach the terminal point of the movement, then you are working with too much "pull"on the tubing. To decrease the amount of resistance or "pull," move closer to the secured end of the tube (use more tube over a shorter distance). To increase the resistance, move farther away from the secured end. Also, work at an angle to the Power Tubing attachment so that each movement can be performed without the tubing becoming tangled or cutting across your body.

As your strength and stamina improve, you can increase the intensity of your workout by:

1. Increasing your distance from the secured end of the tube.
2. Doubling the tubing.
3. Going through more repetitions.
4. Going through a series of exercises more than once (circuits).

OVERHEAD PULLS

Placement of Support System: Bottom of door.
Power Tubing Attachment: Bottom hole of the TENNIS HANDLE.
Starting Position: Grasp the TENNIS HANDLE with both hands, one at the top of the HANDLE and the other at the bottom. Stand erect with arms straight out in front, elbows locked, palms facing down. Keep your body straight and tight.
Action: Slowly pull both arms up and back overhead as far as possible. Try to get your elbow behind your ears. Don't lean back.
Repetitions: 10 Strength; 25 Stamina.

151

BACK PULL

Placement of Support System: Waist height.
Power Tubing Attachment: Bottom hole of the TENNIS HANDLE.
Starting Position: Stand facing the Support System. Grasp the TENNIS HANDLE in your right hand, palm down.
Action: Slowly pull your arms straight back as far as possible, keeping your elbows locked and shoulders back. Don't bend at the waist.
Repetitions: 10 Strength; 25 Stamina; Repeat for left arm.

FRONT PULL

Placement of Support System: Not needed. Hold end of Power Tubing in opposite hand.
Power Tubing Attachment: Bottom hole of the TENNIS HANDLE.
Starting Position: Grasp the TENNIS HANDLE in your dominant hand, hold the end of the Power Tubing in your other hand. Extend both your arms straight in front at shoulder height, elbows locked and palms facing each other.
Action: Slowly pull your arms apart and as far back as possible.
Repetitions: 10 Strength; 25 Stamina.

SHOULDER BACKWARD ROTATION

Placement of Support System: Waist height.

Power Tubing Attachment: Bottom hole of the TENNIS HANDLE.

Starting Position: Stand facing the Support System with the TENNIS HANDLE in your right hand, palm facing the Support System. Raise your upper arm to shoulder height, bend your elbow to 90°.

Action: Keeping your upper arm from your elbow to your shoulder stationary, pull your hand back as far as possible.

Repetitions: 10 Strength; 25 Stamina; Repeat for left arm.

WRIST EXTENSION

Placement of Support System: Bottom of door.

Power Tubing Attachment: Bottom hole of the TENNIS HANDLE.

Starting Position: Grasp the TENNIS HANDLE with your right hand, palm down. Keep your upper arm stationary to your side, elbow bent.

Action: Slowly roll your fist back towards your forearm.

Repetitions: Continue until failure. Repeat with left hand.

Variation: Grasp the TENNIS HANDLE with both hands, one on each side of the Power Tubing. Proceed as above.

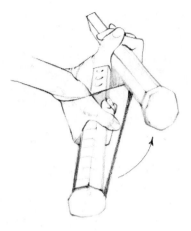

WRIST FLEXION

Placement of Support System: Bottom of door.
Power Tubing Attachment: Bottom hole of TENNIS HANDLE.
Starting Position: Grasp the TENNIS HANDLE with your right hand, with the palm up. Keep the upper arm stationary to your side, elbow bent.
Action: Slowly roll your fist towards your forearms.
Repetitions: Continue to failure. Repeat for left hand.

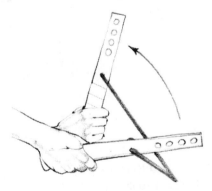

WRIST ABDUCTION

Placement of Support System: Bottom of door.
Power Tubing Attachment: Bottom hole of the TENNIS HANDLE.
Starting Position: Grasp the TENNIS HANDLE with your dominant hand with a comfortable grip. Keep your upper arm stationary to your side.
Action: Slowly, cock your wrist up as far as possible.
Repetitions: Continue until failure.

154

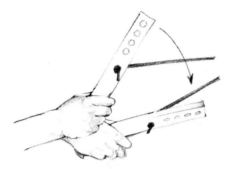

WRIST ADDUCTION

Placement of Support System: Slightly above shoulder height.
Power Tubing Attachment: Bottom hole of the TENNIS HANDLE.
Starting Position: Stand with your back to the Support System. Grasp the TENNIS HANDLE with your dominant hand with a comfortable grip. Keep your upper arm stationary to your side.
Action: Slowly bend your wrist downward as far as possible.
Repetitions: Continue until failure.

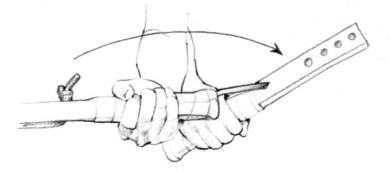

SUPINATION

Placement of Support System: Waist height.
Power Tubing Attachment: Bottom hole of the TENNIS HANDLE.
Starting Position: Stand with your right side to the Support System. Grip the TENNIS HANDLE with your dominant hand, palm up. Keep your upper arm stationary to your side and bend your elbow to 90°.
Action: Slowly roll your wrist over to a palm-down position. Keep your wrist straight.
Repetitions: Continue until failure.

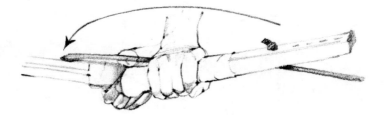

PRONATION

Placement of Support System: Waist height.

Power Tubing Attachment: Bottom hole of TENNIS HANDLE.

Starting Position: Stand with your right side to the Support System. Grasp the TENNIS HANDLE with your dominant hand, palm down. Keep your upper arm stationary to the side and bend your elbow to 90°

Action: Slowly turn your hand to a palm-up position. Keep your wrist straight.

Repetitions: Continue until failure.

SPECIFIC STRENGTH PROGRAMS FOR REHABILITATION

Any injury should be seen by the proper medical personnel before any rehabilitation is started. Your physician may give you some guidelines for when you can start an exercise program. **If the exercise program causes pain, discontinue until you consult your physician.**

A few suggested strength exercises for specific areas are:

Shoulder: (Rotator Cuff)
Backward Rotation
Backpulls
Overhead Pulls
Front Pulls

Elbow/Wrist: (Tennis Elbow)
Wrist Extension/Wrist Flexion
Supination/Pronation
Adduction/Abduction

Chronic Ankle Sprains:
Dorsiflexion
Eversion

Lower Leg Pain (Shin Splints)
Dorsiflexion
Eversion
Inversion

Knee Pain
Hip Flexion
Hip Hyperextension
Hip Adduction
Hip Abduction

APPENDIX

The products mentioned in this chapter are available by writing to:
For NICK BOLLETTIERI TENNIS HANDLE:
    Nick Bollettieri Tennis Handle
    Box 1177
    Wheaton, Illinois 60187
Cost: $19.95 plus $3.00 for shipping and handling. Send Check
or Money Order Only.

For POWERBANDS & Price List:
    SPRI, Products
    501 Thornhill Drive
    Carol Stream, Illinois 60187